English for Listening, Speaking, Reading & Writing

NEW CONNECTION

BRING YOUR ENGLISH TO THE NEXT LEVEL

STUDENT BOOK 1

INTRODUCTION

Welcome to ***NEW CONNECTION*** — *BRING YOUR ENGLISH TO THE NEXT LEVEL.* This is the first book of a series created to propel learners as they take the next step toward fluency. Outstanding English skills will open doors for anyone in today's world. No matter how ambitious a student's learning goals are, the ***NEW CONNECTION*** series will provide the boost he or she needs.

Each unit of ***NEW CONNECTION*** — *BRING YOUR ENGLISH TO THE NEXT LEVEL* follows a set structure designed to encourage students to both expand their skills and put what they have learned into practice. The unit begins with the **Expressions** and **Small Talk** sections, in which common topic-related expressions are introduced and practiced. This is followed by **Words**, a section put together to expand vocabulary and provide a context for its use.

The heart of each unit is the central **Conversation**, which is supported by video. This component uses natural language to introduce certain grammar points, review vocabulary, and provide handy everyday English tips. The **Grammar** segment explains and consolidates the understanding of these new grammar points. The following **Reading** section provides an opportunity for students to really test their comprehension of the material covered while the **Writing** section ensures they can express that understanding.

Each section is designed to build on the last and incorporates both audio support and practical testing. The book structure has a similar, progressive pattern. Each unit develops the lessons of the previous one, preparing the groundwork for the next.

As students progress through the levels, they are constantly encouraged to put what they have learned to use. At the same time, they are presented new challenges. In rising to meet them, students are able to reach the next benchmark in the learning process. By promoting an interest in this process of advancement, ***NEW CONNECTION*** — *BRING YOUR ENGLISH TO THE NEXT LEVEL* helps learners to realize that the sky is the limit.

CONTENTS

CONTENT CHART

Unit	Title	Subject	Conversation	Grammar
1	**Just for Fun**	Hobbies	Let's Go Swimming	Simple Present Tense
2	**Grocery Shopping**	Groceries	At the Supermarket	Count Nouns vs. Non-Count Nouns
3	**Blue Skies**	Weather	Happy in the Rain	Comparatives and Superlatives
4	**The World of Computers**	Computer	Save My Computer!	Coordinating Conjunctions Sensing Verbs
5	**Man's Best Friends**	Pets	The Perfect Pet	Gerunds and Infinitives
6	**At the Department Store**	Shopping	Shopping for Clothes	Imperatives
7	**Daily Life**	Places	Help!	Present Continuous
8	**Out in Nature**	Nature	Nature Walk	Subordinating Conjunctions
9	**On Campus**	School	Test Trouble	The Simple Past
10	**Happy Times**	Special Day	The Big Party	Expressing Time
11	**Food to Go**	Food	Breakfast Sandwich	Adjectives
12	**On the Road**	Travel	Summer Work and Play	Future: Be going to

	Reading	Writing
❙ Statements ❙ Third Person Singular ❙ Yes / No Questions ❙ Wh- Questions	Hobbies for Your Health	Schedules
❙ Statements ❙ Plural Count Nouns	Fruit Talks	Coupons
❙ Regular Adjectives ❙ Irregular Adjectives ❙ Functions	Crazy Weather	Local Weather
	The Internet in Your Pocket	Computer Use
❙ Form ❙ Usage ❙ Verbs with Gerunds / Infinitives	Want a Bigger Pet?	Animal Profiles
❙ Forms ❙ Functions ❙ The Imperative with *Let's*	A New World of Shopping	Directions
❙ Statements ❙ Yes / No Questions ❙ Wh- Questions ❙ Be + Verb + -ing	Everyday Training of an Astronaut	Blogs
	Wonders of the World	Travel Websites
❙ Be Verbs ❙ Verbs	Bedroom Classroom	Find a Tutor
❙ Prepositions ❙ Expressions	The World's Biggest Party	Invitation Letters
❙ Positions ❙ Types	Your Size and French Fries	Eating Habits
❙ Statements ❙ Yes / No Questions ❙ Wh- Questions ❙ Other Tenses for the Future	The First Hotel in Outer Space	Travel Plans

LEARNING OVERVIEW

Words
provides a list of words with photos and audio support to build students' vocabulary knowledge to understand upcoming activities.

Act It Out
helps students understand the key expressions and words by practicing short dialogues.

Listen Up
checks students' understanding of the words they have learned through listening comprehension questions.

Expressions
provides useful expressions with audio support to further students' understanding of the topic.

Conversation
includes a video clip helping students understand the content.

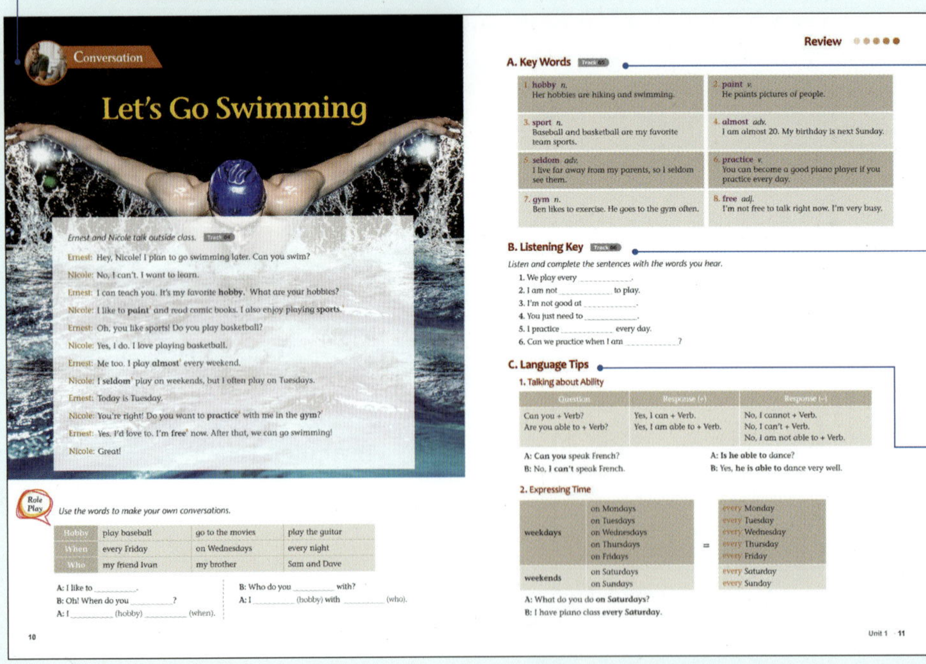

Key Words
introduces additional words to expand students' vocabulary.

Listening Key
checks students' understanding of the passage through listening comprehension questions.

Language Tips
provides everyday English usage and sentence structure.

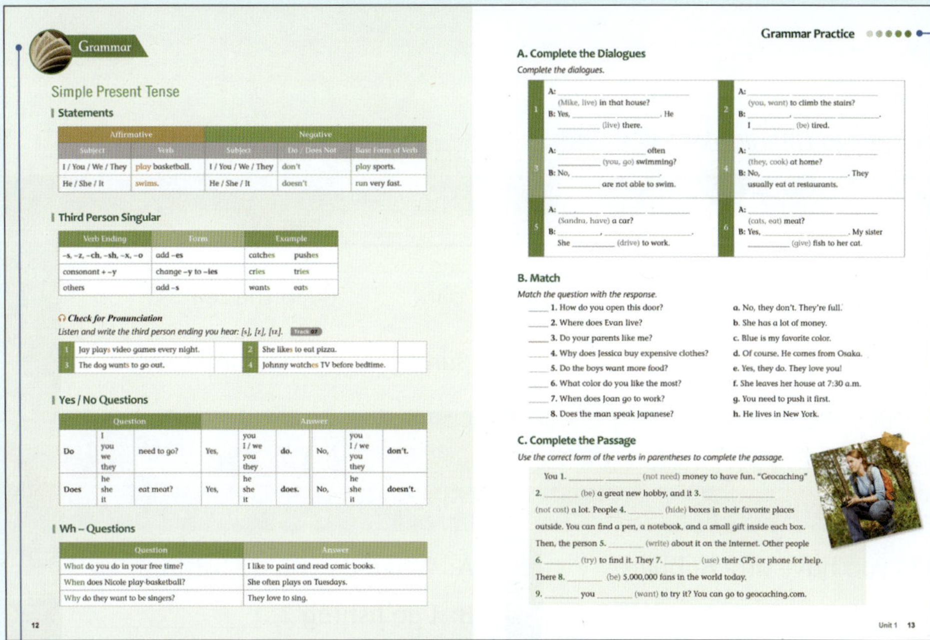

Grammar Practice

enables students to practice grammar in context to enhance accuracy and fluency.

Grammar

presents essential grammar to build overall accuracy.

Reading

enables students to broaden their knowledge through interesting articles.

After You Read

confirms students' understanding of the passage.

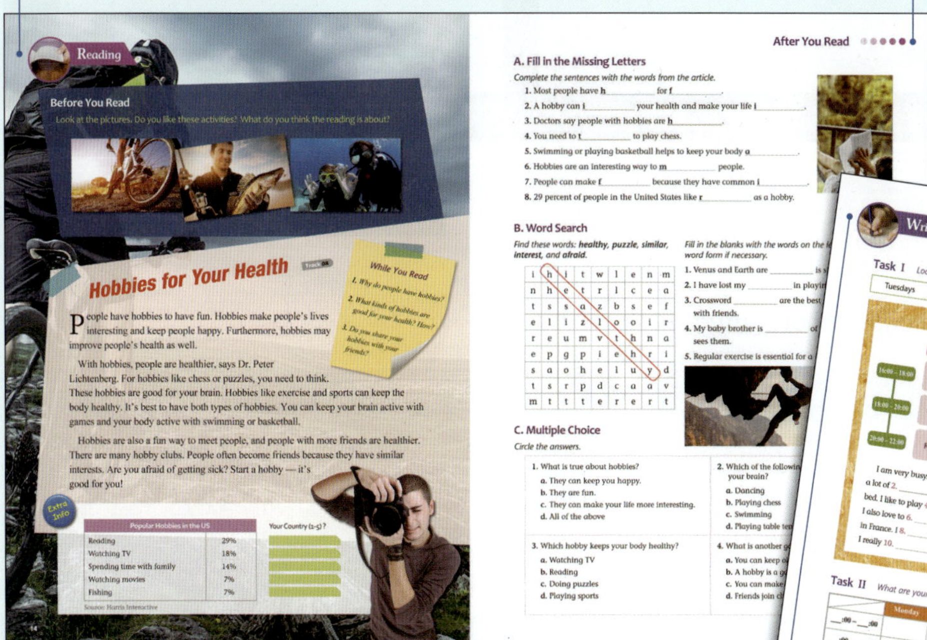

Writing

provides an opportunity for students to practice acquired language in authentic discourse using personalized content.

UNIT 1 Just for Fun

1. What do you do in your free time?
2. Which sports do you like?
3. What interests do you share with your friends?

Expressions

Listen and write the correct letters in the blanks. Track 01

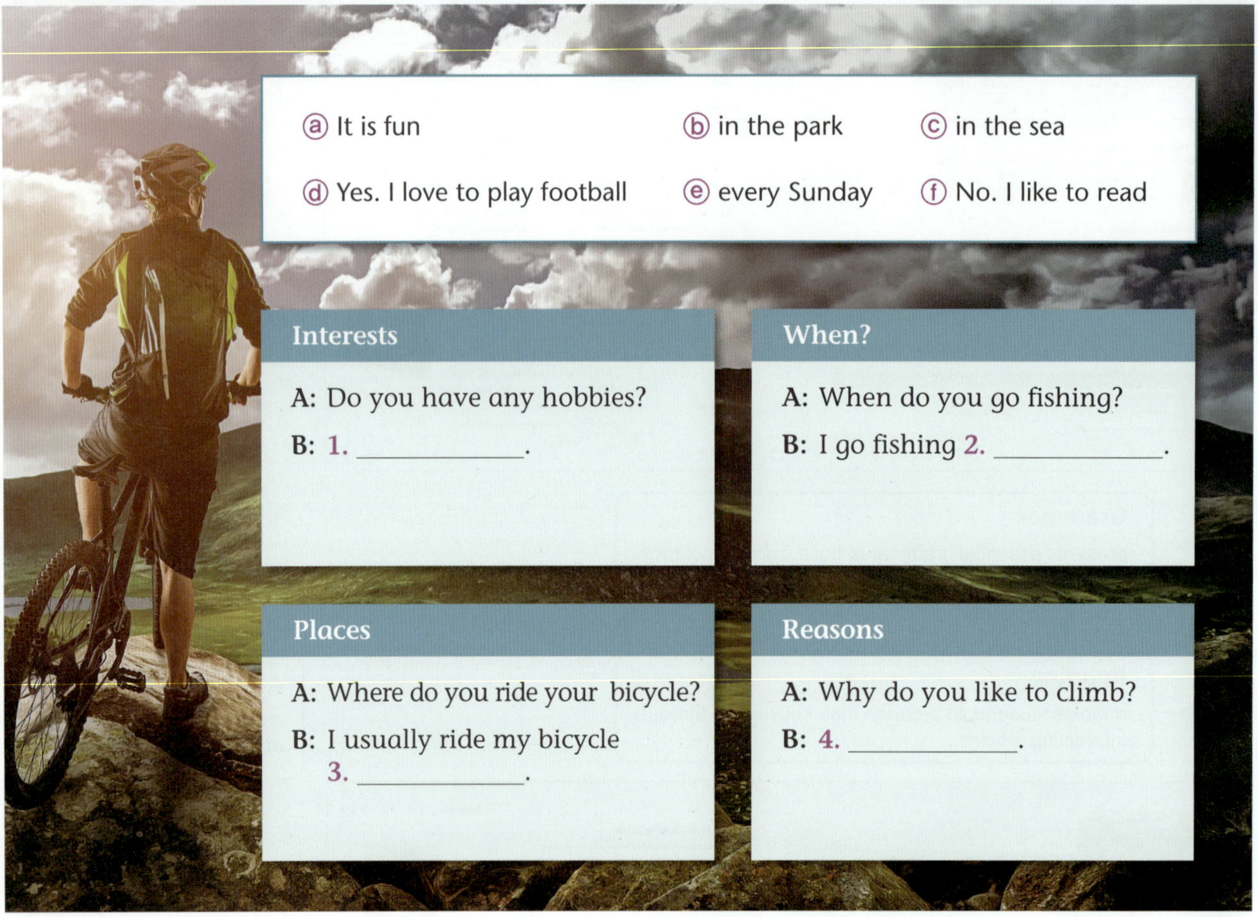

ⓐ It is fun ⓑ in the park ⓒ in the sea

ⓓ Yes. I love to play football ⓔ every Sunday ⓕ No. I like to read

Interests

A: Do you have any hobbies?

B: 1. __________.

When?

A: When do you go fishing?

B: I go fishing 2. __________.

Places

A: Where do you ride your bicycle?

B: I usually ride my bicycle 3. __________.

Reasons

A: Why do you like to climb?

B: 4. __________.

Small Talk

Practice the dialogues above using these expressions.

Interests

I like to play tennis.
I enjoy swimming.
I go to the movies with my friends.

When?

every week
on weekends
on Thursdays

Places

on the street
near my house
by the river

Reasons

I like being outside.
My friends all like to climb.
It's good exercise.

Words

Listen and repeat the words. Track 02

1 play chess *phr.*

2 exercise *v.*

3 play video games *phr.*

4 play the guitar *phr.*

5 swim *v.*

6 cook *v.*

7 read comic books *phr.*

8 see plays *phr.*

Act It Out

*Practice talking about **hobbies** with a partner.*

Question	Response
What are your hobbies?	I like + Verb + -ing / to... I enjoy + Verb + -ing. Verb + -ing + is my favorite hobby.

Look at the pictures and fill in the blanks.

1. Liz enjoys ________ ________ with her boyfriend.

2. ________ ________ ________ is Nancy and her brother's ________ hobby.

Question	Response			
Do you . . .?	I **always** . . . I **often** . . . I **sometimes** . . .	100% 80% 50%	I **seldom** . . . I **never** . . .	20% 0%

Listen Up

Listen and complete the sentences with the words you hear. Track 03

1. Ken often goes to the theater. His favorite __________ is *Hamlet*.
2. Jimmy likes to __________ and read __________ __________.
3. Karen feels happy when she plays the __________. She __________ misses practice.

Conversation

Let's Go Swimming

Ernest and Nicole talk outside class. Track 04

Ernest: Hey, Nicole! I plan to go swimming later. Can you swim?

Nicole: No, I can't. I want to learn.

Ernest: I can teach you. It's my favorite **hobby**.[1] What are your hobbies?

Nicole: I like to **paint**[2] and read comic books. I also enjoy playing **sports**.[3]

Ernest: Oh, you like sports! Do you play basketball?

Nicole: Yes, I do. I love playing basketball.

Ernest: Me too. I play **almost**[4] every weekend.

Nicole: I **seldom**[5] play on weekends, but I often play on Tuesdays.

Ernest: Today is Tuesday.

Nicole: You're right! Do you want to **practice**[6] with me in the **gym**?[7]

Ernest: Yes. I'd love to. I'm **free**[8] now. After that, we can go swimming!

Nicole: Great!

Role Play *Use the words to make your own conversations.*

Hobby	play baseball	go to the movies	play the guitar
When	every Friday	on Wednesdays	every night
Who	my friend Ivan	my brother	Sam and Dave

A: I like to ___________.
B: Oh! When do you ___________?
A: I ___________ (hobby) ___________ (when).

B: Who do you ___________ with?
A: I ___________ (hobby) with ___________ (who).

A. Key Words

Track 05

1. **hobby** *n.* Her hobbies are hiking and swimming.	2. **paint** *v.* He paints pictures of people.
3. **sport** *n.* Baseball and basketball are my favorite team sports.	4. **almost** *adv.* I am almost 20. My birthday is next Sunday.
5. **seldom** *adv.* I live far away from my parents, so I seldom see them.	6. **practice** *v.* You can become a good piano player if you practice every day.
7. **gym** *n.* Ben likes to exercise. He goes to the gym often.	8. **free** *adj.* I'm not free to talk right now. I'm very busy.

B. Listening Key

Track 06

Listen and complete the sentences with the words you hear.

1. We play every ____________.
2. I am not ____________ to play.
3. I'm not good at ____________.
4. You just need to ____________.
5. I practice ____________ every day.
6. Can we practice when I am ____________?

C. Language Tips

1. Talking about Ability

Question	Response (+)	Response (–)
Can you + Verb? Are you able to + Verb?	Yes, I can + Verb. Yes, I am able to + Verb.	No, I cannot + Verb. No, I can't + Verb. No, I am not able to + Verb.

A: **Can you** speak French?
B: No, **I can't** speak French.

A: **Is he able to** dance?
B: Yes, **he is able to** dance very well.

2. Expressing Time

weekdays	on Mondays on Tuesdays on Wednesdays on Thursdays on Fridays	=	every Monday every Tuesday every Wednesday every Thursday every Friday
weekends	on Saturdays on Sundays		every Saturday every Sunday

A: What do you do **on Saturdays**?
B: I have piano class **every Saturday**.

Grammar

Simple Present Tense

Statements

Affirmative		Negative		
Subject	Verb	Subject	Do / Does Not	Base Form of Verb
I / You / We / They	play basketball.	I / You / We / They	don't	play sports.
He / She / It	swims.	He / She / It	doesn't	run very fast.

Third Person Singular

Verb Ending	Form	Example	
–s, –z, –ch, –sh, –x, –o	add –es	catches	pushes
consonant + –y	change –y to –ies	cries	tries
others	add –s	wants	eats

Check for Pronunciation

Listen and write the third person ending you hear: [s], [z], [ɪz]. Track 07

1	Jay plays video games every night.		2	She likes to eat pizza.	
3	The dog wants to go out.		4	Johnny watches TV before bedtime.	

Yes / No Questions

Question			Answer					
Do	I you we they	need to go?	Yes,	you I / we you they	**do.**	No,	you I / we you they	**don't.**
Does	he she it	eat meat?	Yes,	he she it	**does.**	No,	he she it	**doesn't.**

Wh – Questions

Question	Answer
What do you do in your free time?	I like to paint and read comic books.
When does Nicole play basketball?	She often plays on Tuesdays.
Why do they want to be singers?	They love to sing.

A. Complete the Dialogues

Complete the dialogues.

1	A: ________ ________ ________ (Mike, live) in that house? B: Yes, ________ ________. He ________ (live) there.	2	A: ________ ________ ________ (you, want) to climb the stairs? B: ________, ________ ________. I ________ (be) tired.
3	A: ________ ________ often ________ (you, go) swimming? B: No, ________ ________. We are not able to swim.	4	A: ________ ________ ________ (they, cook) at home? B: No, ________ ________. They usually eat at restaurants.
5	A: ________ ________ ________ (Sandra, have) a car? B: ________, ________ ________. She ________ (drive) to work.	6	A: ________ ________ ________ (cats, eat) meat? B: Yes, ________ ________. My sister ________ (give) fish to her cat.

B. Match

Match the question with the response.

_____ **1.** How do you open this door?
_____ **2.** Where does Evan live?
_____ **3.** Do your parents like me?
_____ **4.** Why does Jessica buy expensive clothes?
_____ **5.** Do the boys want more food?
_____ **6.** What color do you like the most?
_____ **7.** When does Joan go to work?
_____ **8.** Does the man speak Japanese?

a. No, they don't. They're full.
b. She has a lot of money.
c. Blue is my favorite color.
d. Of course. He comes from Osaka.
e. Yes, they do. They love you!
f. She leaves her house at 7:30 a.m.
g. You need to push it first.
h. He lives in New York.

C. Complete the Passage

Use the correct form of the verbs in parentheses to complete the passage.

You **1.** ________ ________ (not need) money to have fun. "Geocaching" **2.** ________ (be) a great new hobby, and it **3.** ________ ________ (not cost) a lot. People **4.** ________ (hide) boxes in their favorite places outside. You can find a pen, a notebook, and a small gift inside each box. Then, the person **5.** ________ (write) about it on the Internet. Other people **6.** ________ (try) to find it. They **7.** ________ (use) their GPS or phone for help. There **8.** ________ (be) 5,000,000 fans in the world today. **9.** ________ you ________ (want) to try it? You can go to geocaching.com.

Reading

Before You Read

Look at the pictures. Do you like these activities? What do you think the reading is about?

Hobbies for Your Health

Track 08

While You Read

1. Why do people have hobbies?

2. What kinds of hobbies are good for your health? How?

3. Do you share your hobbies with your friends?

People have hobbies to have fun. Hobbies make people's lives interesting and keep people happy. Furthermore, hobbies may improve people's health as well.

With hobbies, people are healthier, says Dr. Peter Lichtenberg. For hobbies like chess or puzzles, you need to think. These hobbies are good for your brain. Hobbies like exercise and sports can keep the body healthy. It's best to have both types of hobbies. You can keep your brain active with games and your body active with swimming or basketball.

Hobbies are also a fun way to meet people, and people with more friends are healthier. There are many hobby clubs. People often become friends because they have similar interests. Are you afraid of getting sick? Start a hobby — it's good for you!

Extra Info

Popular Hobbies in the U.S.	
Reading	29%
Watching TV	18%
Spending time with family	14%
Watching movies	7%
Fishing	7%

Source: Harris Interactive

Your Country (1-5)?

A. Fill in the Missing Letters

Complete the sentences with the words from the article.

1. Most people have **h**__________ for **f**__________.
2. A hobby can **i**__________ your health and make your life **i**__________.
3. Doctors say people with hobbies are **h**__________.
4. You need to **t**__________ to play chess.
5. Swimming or playing basketball helps to keep your body **a**__________.
6. Hobbies are an interesting way to **m**__________ people.
7. People can make **f**__________ because they have common **i**__________.
8. 29 percent of people in the United States like **r**__________ as a hobby.

B. Word Search

*Find these words: **healthy**, **puzzle**, **similar**, **interest**, and **afraid**.*

i	h	i	t	w	l	e	n	m
n	h	e	t	r	l	c	e	a
t	s	s	a	z	b	s	e	f
e	l	i	z	l	o	o	i	r
r	e	u	m	v	t	h	n	a
e	p	g	p	i	e	h	r	i
s	a	o	h	e	l	u	y	d
t	s	r	p	d	c	a	a	v
m	t	t	t	e	r	e	r	t

Fill in the blanks with the words on the left. Change the word form if necessary.

1. Venus and Earth are __________ in size, mass and density.
2. I have lost my __________ in playing online games.
3. Crossword __________ are the best way to spend time with friends.
4. My baby brother is __________ of dogs. He cries when he sees them.
5. Regular exercise is essential for a __________ lifestyle.

C. Multiple Choice

Circle the answers.

1. What is true about hobbies?
   a. They can keep you happy.
   b. They are fun.
   c. They can make your life more interesting.
   d. All of the above

2. Which of the following is good exercise for your brain?
   a. Dancing
   b. Playing chess
   c. Swimming
   d. Playing table tennis

3. Which hobby keeps your body healthy?
   a. Watching TV
   b. Reading
   c. Doing puzzles
   d. Playing sports

4. What is another good thing about hobbies?
   a. You can keep old friends.
   b. A hobby is a good friend.
   c. You can make new friends.
   d. Friends join clubs together.

UNIT 2

Grocery Shopping

1. Where do you shop for groceries?
2. What do you buy every week?
3. Is it cheap to buy food in convenience stores?

Expressions

Listen and write the correct letters in the blanks. Track 09

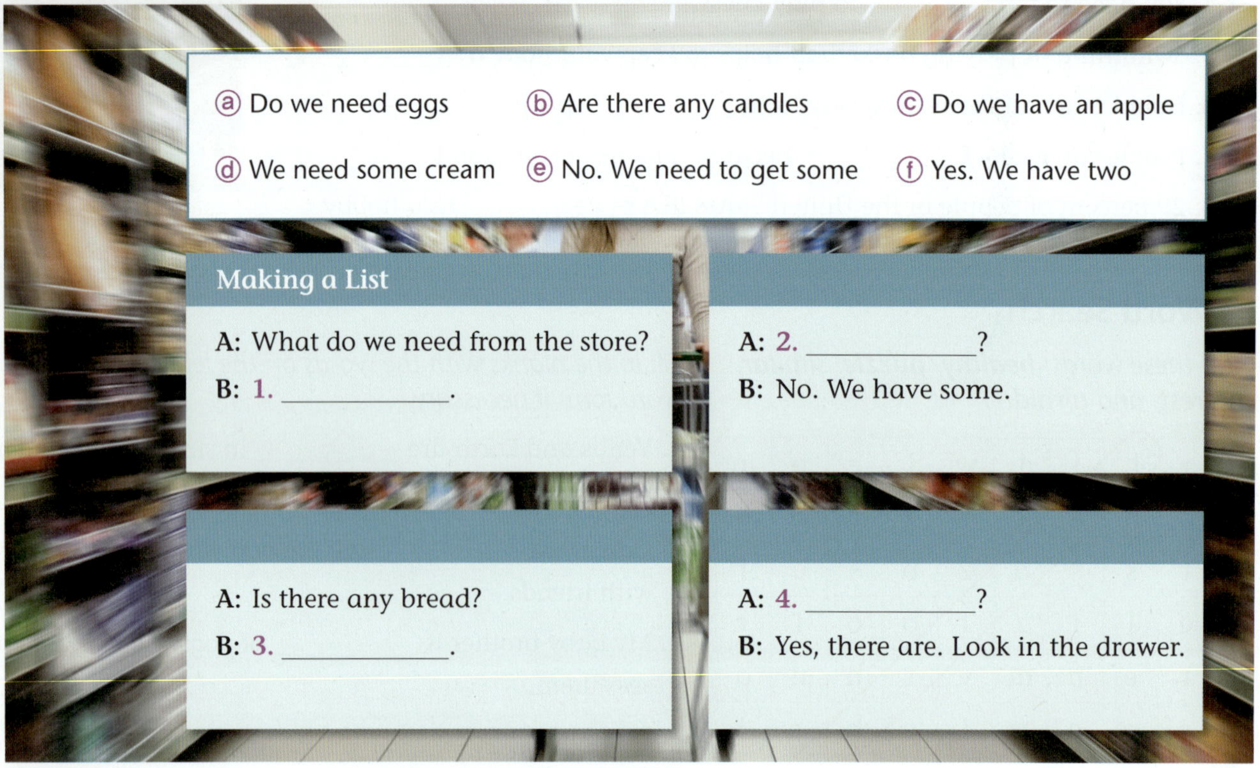

ⓐ Do we need eggs ⓑ Are there any candles ⓒ Do we have an apple

ⓓ We need some cream ⓔ No. We need to get some ⓕ Yes. We have two

Making a List

A: What do we need from the store?
B: 1. ____________.

A: 2. ____________?
B: No. We have some.

A: Is there any bread?
B: 3. ____________.

A: 4. ____________?
B: Yes, there are. Look in the drawer.

Small Talk

Practice the dialogues above using these expressions.

What do we need from the store?

What do we need to buy?
What is on our shopping list?

We need some cream.

We don't need anything.
We need some apples.
We need to buy some water.

Do we need eggs?

Do we need any apples?
Do we need to buy soup?
Should we get some milk?

No. We have some.

Yes. We should buy some.
No. We don't need to buy eggs.

Is there any bread?

Are there any noodles?
Do we have any rice?

Look in the drawer.

They are in the drawer.
Check the drawer.

Words

Listen and repeat the words. Track 10

1 mop *n.*

2 soap *n.*

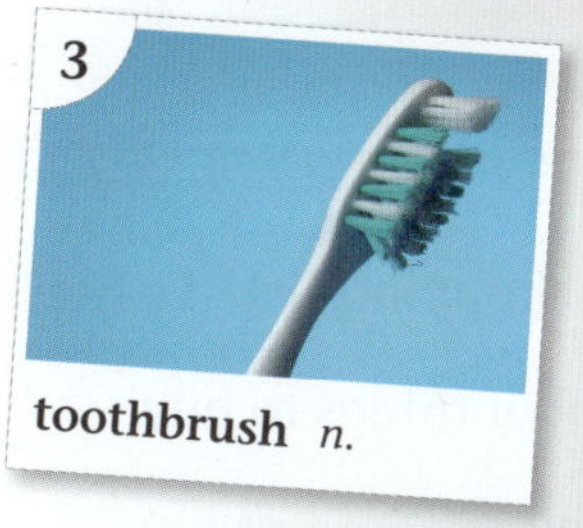
3 toothbrush *n.*

4 doughnut *n.*

5 vegetables *n.*

6 toilet paper *n.*

7 sandwich *n.*

8 meat *n.*

Act It Out

*Practice talking about **shopping** with a partner.*

Question	Response
Where do you buy . . . ?	I like to buy . . . at the supermarket. I usually go to the convenience store. I go to the market.
How much does the . . . cost?	It costs $2.50. It's $1.80.
How much do the . . . cost?	They cost $6.40. They're $3.10 each.

Listen Up

Task I *Put the letters in the right order.*

Shopping List	
psoa ▶	____________
estableevg ▶	____________
amte ▶	____________
ohtotrbsuh ▶	____________
leitot rapep ▶	____________
hugsdotun ▶	____________

Task II *Listen and fill in the blanks.* Track 11

1. Josh wants to make a ____________.
2. He needs some ____________.
3. Molly wants a ____________.
4. They also need ____________, soap, and ____________ paper.
5. The ____________ at the supermarket ____________ $2.40 a pack.

Conversation

At the Supermarket

Joanne and Esther are at the supermarket. Track 12

Joanne: Do you have the shopping **list**,[1] Esther?

Esther: Yes. We have a lot of things to buy.

Joanne: What's the first thing?

Esther: The first thing is toilet paper. Here it is!

Joanne: We need some **jam**[2] too. I like to eat **toast**[3] and jam for breakfast.

Esther: The next thing is **cheese**.[4] The cheese is over there.

Joanne: I already have it. What **else**[5] do we need?

Esther: We need a big bottle of water and some onions.

Joanne: Here's the water. I can **carry**[6] it. Where are the onions?

Esther: The vegetable **section**[7] is over here. I can get the onions.

Joanne: I also want a bar of chocolate.

Esther: It's not on the list, but I want some chocolate too. Get two bars.

Joanne: OK. Let's **pay**[8] now!

Role Play

Match the food to the group. Use the words to make your own conversation.

some bread • two apples • a bag of onions

fruit • bakery • vegetable

a papaya • a pumpkin • some carrots • a cake

A: I want to buy ________________.

B: It's / They're in the ________________ section.

A: Where is that?

B: It's beside the ________________ section.

A: Thank you.

B: You're welcome.

A. Key Words Track 13

1. **list** *n.*
Write a list of your favorite books.

2. **jam** *n.*
Jam tastes good on bread.

3. **toast** *n.*
You need bread, milk, and eggs to make French toast.

4. **cheese** *n.*
Some cheese smell bad.

5. **else** *adv.*
I don't like hamburgers. Is there anything else to eat?

6. **carry** *v.*
The mother always carries her child in her arms.

7. **section** *n.*
This section of the city is very rich.

8. **pay** *v.*
You need to pay $76 to enter Disneyland.

B. Listening Key Track 14

Listen and put the words in the right order.

1. you / Can / a / get / Eric? / basket, ▶ ____________________
2. over / is / The / section / dairy / there. ▶ ____________________
3. cream. / need / buy / Next, / we / to / ice ▶ ____________________
4. do / we / What / need? / else ▶ ____________________
5. last / is / The / jam. / thing ▶ ____________________
6. we / need / Now / pay. / to ▶ ____________________

C. Language Tips

1. Lists

The	first next last	thing on the list is . . .

First, Next, Last,	we need to buy . . . we should get . . .

Practice the sentence patterns with the items below.

tomatoes	cookies	butter	eggs

2. Where Is It?

Question	Response	
	Near	Far
Where is the bread?	Here it is. Here is the bread.	There it is. There is the bread.
Where are the bananas?	Here they are. Here are the bananas.	There they are. There are the bananas.

Grammar

Count Nouns vs. Non-Count Nouns

Statements

Count Nouns

	Singular			Plural		
Affirmative	I need	a an	basket. egg.	You can buy	two a few some many a lot of	sandwiches. candles.
Negative	I don't have	a an	toothbrush. onion.	I don't want	two any many a lot of	oranges. doughnuts.

Non-Count Nouns

Affirmative	Give me	a little some a lot of	jam. cheese.
Negative	She doesn't drink	any much a lot of	milk. tea.

Usage Note

For non-count nouns and singular count nouns, use **there is**. For plural count nouns, use **there are**.

For Example:
There is water on the table.
There are 40 students in my class.

Plural Count Nouns

	Noun Ending	Form	Example	
Regular Plurals	–s, –sh, –ch, –x, –z	add –es	buses	foxes
	consonant + –y	change –y to –ies	cities	ladies
	–o	add –es or –s	potatoes	photos
	others	add –s	mops	doughnuts
Irregular Plurals	tooth → teeth	man → men	child → children	

Check for Pronunciation

Listen and write the ending of the plural noun you hear: [s], [z], [ɪz]. Track 15

1	Bob has many friends.		2	I don't have any classes today.	
3	There are 12 months in a year.		4	The island has beautiful beaches.	

A. Fill in the Blanks

Use the word choices given to complete the sentences. For some questions, more than one answer is correct.

a
an
the
a few
X

1. There is ________ man over there. He's our new neighbor.
2. I need ________ more minutes. Please wait for me.
3. Harrison has ________ news for you.
4. I have to go to ________ library this afternoon.
5. We saw ________ old lady dancing on the street.

many
much
a lot of
any
a little

6. I don't like sweet things. I only want ________ sugar in my coffee.
7. Sara doesn't read ________ books. She only reads one or two every year.
8. We don't have ________ money. We just have ten dollars.
9. There are ________ people in the park. There are more than 2,000.
10. Do you have ________ questions? I can answer them now.

B. Match

Match the question/statement with the response.

_____ 1. Do you need some help?
_____ 2. How much time do you have?
_____ 3. Is there any space in your bag?
_____ 4. We need to bring a lot of warm clothes.
_____ 5. Do we have a picture of her?
_____ 6. We don't need any oranges.
_____ 7. Do you need an answer today?
_____ 8. How much TV do you watch?

a. Yes. You can put your camera in.
b. OK. I can put them back.
c. I watch about three hours a week.
d. I have an hour.
e. No. I can do it.
f. Yes. Here it is.
g. We don't need warm clothes. It's really hot there.
h. No. You can tell me tomorrow.

C. Complete the Passage

Look at the picture and use the word choices given to complete the passage. For some questions, more than one answer is correct.

some	a little	the	any	many	a lot of	a	much

This is **1.** ________ painting by Henri Matisse. **2.** ________ painting is from 1897. On **3.** ________ table, there are **4.** ________ types of fruit and **5.** ____________ flowers. There are also three bottles of wine and **6.** ____________ water. There is one chair, but there aren't **7.** ________ guests. There is **8.** ____________ fruit but not **9.** ____________ food for dinner. The woman has a lot of things to do before **10.** ________ guests come!

Dinner Table

Reading

Before You Read

Look at the pictures. Which is your favorite? What do you think the reading is about?

Fruit Talks

Track 16

While You Read

1. *Do you know any meanings of fruit?*
2. *What is a lucky fruit in Greece?*

Fruit is delicious and healthy, but sometimes it can be more than just food. Cultures around the world give meanings to different fruits.

To the Greeks, apples are a symbol of love and beauty. For the Norse and the Celts, they bring long life. To the Chinese, apples are a sign of peace.

Cherries also have many meanings. In England, they are lucky for farmers. Cherry blossoms represent beauty to the Japanese.

Pomegranates are another important fruit. People bring them to weddings in Greece. They're good luck. In China, they suggest lots of children because they have so many seeds.

Many fruits have interesting meanings. Next time you enjoy a natural snack, think about its meaning.

Extra Info

What do these fruits mean?

Fruit	Meaning	Culture
Strawberry	Spring and new life	Native American
Pineapple	Welcome	American and European
Tangerine	Good luck	Chinese

A. Fill in the Missing Letters

Complete the sentences with the words from the article.

1. Fruit is a natural **s**____________. It is **d**____________ and healthy.
2. Fruit is more than just **f**____________. It has different **m**____________ in different cultures.
3. Apples mean **p**____________ in Chinese culture.
4. Cherries are **l**____________ for **f**____________ in England.
5. People bring pomegranates to **w**____________ in Greece.
6. Pomegranates have lots of **s**____________. They are a sign of many **c**____________ in China.

B. Classification

Match the fruit with the culture and the meaning.

a. apple	**b.** cherry	**c.** pomegranate	**d.** pineapple	**e.** strawberry

	Culture	Meaning
1.________	English	good luck for farmers
2.________	Native American	new life
3.________	Norse and Celtic	long life
4.________	American	welcome
5.________	Greek	good luck

C. Multiple Choice

Circle the answers.

1. Which of these is NOT true of fruit?
   - **a.** It tastes great.
   - **b.** It is healthy.
   - **c.** Some fruits have interesting meanings.
   - **d.** It is Greek.

2. Which fruit has the most seeds?
   - **a.** Oranges
   - **b.** Pomegranates
   - **c.** Pears
   - **d.** Apples

3. What do cherry blossoms mean to the Japanese?
   - **a.** Luck
   - **b.** Beauty
   - **c.** Love
   - **d.** Peace

4. What is another appropriate title for the article?
   - **a.** Fruit Is Good for You
   - **b.** China Has a Lot of Fruit
   - **c.** Fruits Have Many Meanings
   - **d.** Pomegranates Have a Lot of Seeds

UNIT

3 Blue Skies

1. Do you watch the weather report?
2. What kind of weather do you like the most?
3. What is the worst kind of weather?

Expressions

Listen and write the correct letters in the blanks. Track 17

ⓐ I like the rain ⓑ Is it snowy ⓒ What is it like outside

ⓓ It's a windy season ⓔ My favorite season is spring ⓕ Yes. It's a beautiful day

Weather

A: 1. ____________?

B: It's rainy.

Seasons

A: What season do you like the most?

B: 2. ____________.

Types

A: What's your favorite weather?

B: 3. ____________.

Good or Bad?

A: Is it nice outside?

B: 4. ____________.

Small Talk *Practice the dialogues above using these expressions.*

Weather

What's the weather like?

How is the weather?

Seasons

I like summer best.

Fall is my favorite season.

My favorite season is winter.

Types

I love sunny days.

My favorite weather is sunny.

Cloudy days are the best.

Good or Bad?

It's a lovely day.

The skies are clear and blue.

The weather is terrible.

Words

Listen and repeat the words. Track 18

1 
snow *n.*

2 
storm *n.*

3 
wind *n.*

4 
cloudy *adj.*

5 
sunny *adj.*

6 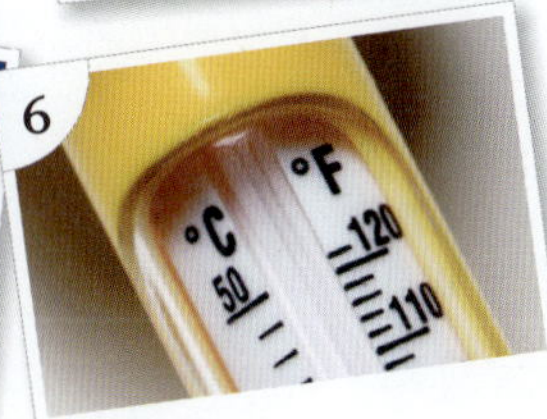

degree *n.*

7 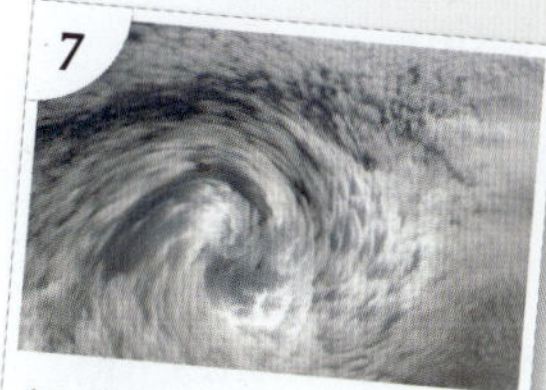
typhoon *n.*

8 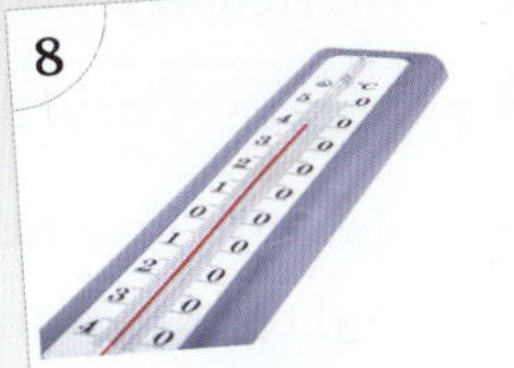
temperature *n.*

Act It Out

Practice talking about ***weather*** *with a partner.*

Question	Response
Is it hot in your country?	Yes. It's really hot in summer. Yes. It's very sunny too. Yes. The temperature is above 40 degrees sometimes. No. We have a lot of snow.
What is the weather like in your country?	We have typhoons from June to October. It is often cloudy. There are a lot of storms. The wind is very strong.

Listen Up

Listen and fill in the chart. Track 19

sunny 19 24 windy cloudy 32

City	 New York	 Tokyo	 Seoul
Temperature	______	______	______
Weather	______	______	______

Conversation

Happy in the Rain

Lizzy and Henry meet on the street. Track 20

Lizzy: Hi, Henry! It's cold today.

Henry: I **agree**,[1] Lizzy. **Luckily**,[2] there is no rain. I don't like the rain.

Lizzy: Really? I love **rainy**[3] days. I like to carry a nice umbrella. You can see **rainbows**[4] sometimes too.

Henry: Hmm. I still hate the rain. I **prefer**[5] **dry**[6] weather. I'm from California.

Lizzy: Oh? Is it warmer in California than it is here?

Henry: The winter is warmer. In summer, it's about the **same**[7] temperature.

Lizzy: That's nice. It's still warm enough for me here in winter. What's the warmest place on **earth**?[8]

Henry: There's a place in Ethiopia. It's 35 degrees **all year round**.[9]

Lizzy: Wow! That's too hot for me. I don't want to live there.

Role Play *Use the words to make your own conversations.*

rainy / sunny / snowy / clear / windy
spring / summer / fall / winter
warm / cold / dry / wet

A: Do you like ____________ (weather) days?
B: ____________.
A: Do you prefer ____________ or ____________ (season)?
B: I like ____________.
A: What is the weather in your city like?
B: It's ____________ in my city.

A. Key Words Track 21

1. **agree** *v.* I don't agree with you. You're wrong.	2. **luckily** *adv.* Luckily, our house is safe from the typhoon.
3. **rainy** *adj.* On rainy days, I stay at home.	4. **rainbow** *n.* There are seven colors in a rainbow.
5. **prefer** *v.* I prefer London to New York. London is more fun.	6. **dry** *adj.* It's very dry in Las Vegas. It seldom rains.
7. **same** *adj.* My bag is the same color as Penny's.	8. **earth** *n.* Russia is the biggest country on earth.
9. **all year round** *phr.* The restaurant is open all year round.	

B. Listening Key Track 22

Listen and complete the sentences with the words you hear.

1. Helen is from the ____________.
2. Helen doesn't like the ____________ in Canada. It is ____________ cold for her.
3. Hector ____________ warmer climates. Helen ____________ with him.
4. It is too ____________ in Singapore. It's not ____________ enough.
5. It's dry and ____________ in Libya ____________ ____________ ____________.

C. Language Tips

1. Enough vs. Too

enough (positive)	It's warm enough for me here. (I am not cold.) I am full enough. (I am not hungry.)
too (negative)	That is too complicated for me. (That is not easy enough.) My shoes are too small. (They're not big enough.)

Usage Note

We use the sentence pattern **too + adjective/adverb + to...** to mean undesirable excess.

For Example:

I am **too tired to run.** (I am tired. I cannot run.)
The box is **too heavy to carry.** (The box is very heavy. I can't carry it.)

2. Your Home Country

Question	Response	
Where are you from? Where do you come from?	I'm from + (*country*).	I'm from Germany.
	I come from + (*country*).	I come from the U.S.
	I am + (*country adjective*).	I am French.

Grammar

Comparatives and Superlatives

Regular Adjectives

Syllable	Adjective Ending	Comparative	Superlative	Example
one	–e	add –**r**	add –**st**	close-closer-closest
	one vowel and one consonant	repeat the consonant, add –**er**	repeat the consonant, add –**est**	hot-hotter-hottest
	others	add –**er**	add –**est**	cold-colder-coldest
two	–y	change –**y** to –**ier**	change –**y** to –**iest**	lazy-lazier-laziest
three or more	all forms	add **more**	add **most**	beautiful-more beautiful-most beautiful

Usage Note

Some two-syllable adjectives can be used with **–er** / **–est** or **more** / **most**.

Adjective	Comparative	Superlative	Adjective	Comparative	Superlative
quiet	quieter	quietest	friendly	friendlier	friendliest
	more quiet	most quiet		more friendly	most friendly

Irregular Adjectives

Adjective	Comparative	Superlative	Adjective	Comparative	Superlative
good	better	best	little	less	least
bad	worse	worst	many / much	more	most

Functions

	Function	Example
Comparative (use **than**)	compare two things	I am taller than my younger brother. A Ferrari is more expensive than a BMW. The country is quieter than the city.
Superlative (use **the**)	compare things in a group	Ben is the smartest student in the class. This is the most beautiful park in town. Who is the best player on the team?

A. Fill in the Blanks

Write the correct form of the adjectives to complete the sentences.

1. Tokyo is the __________ (big) city in Japan.
2. John's work is __________ (good) than Neil's.
3. Which is __________ (fresh), this salad or that one?
4. Kevin is rich. He has the __________ (much) money in this town.
5. These are the __________ (comfortable) seats in the house.
6. My dad has __________ (little) hair than my mother.
7. Will is the __________ (happy) person on the team.

B. Match

Look at the chart and put the words in the correct order.

	China	The United States	Japan
Land Area	9,327,480 sq km	9,147,420 sq km	364,500 sq km
People	1,300,000,000	298,000,000	127,000,000
Internet Users	31.5%	78.1%	78.2%
Height (male)	168 cm	176 cm	171 cm

Sources: NationMaster.com, World Bank

1. are / Males / tallest. / the U.S. / the / from
   ▶ ______________________________
2. most / has / people. / the / China
   ▶ ______________________________
3. than / people / in China. / the Internet / in the U.S. / More / use
   ▶ ______________________________
4. than / Japan. / bigger / is / China
   ▶ ______________________________

C. Complete the Passage

Use the correct form of the words in parentheses to complete the passage.

Hi! I'm Alex and I'm 15. I am the **1.** __________ (young) child in my family. I have two **2.** __________ (old) brothers. Alan is 18 and David is 21. I'm **3.** __________ (short) than both of them. At 175 centimeters, David is the **4.** __________ (tall) of the three of us. He weighs 64 kilograms. Alan is almost as tall as David, but he is much **5.** __________ (thin). He's 172 centimeters, but he's only 58 kilograms. I'm the **6.** __________ (light) at 49 kilograms.

Reading

Before You Read

Look at the pictures. Where are these places? What do you think the reading is about?

Crazy Weather

Track 23

While You Read

1. What is the sunniest place on earth?
2. What is the coldest place?

Do you like sunny weather? Yuma, Arizona, is the sunniest place on earth. It's sunny for 4,050 hours each year. That's over 11 hours a day! The temperature can go up to 50 degrees Celsius too. It's hot, but it's very dry. If you like rain, you can go to Lloró, Colombia. It's the wettest place in the world. It gets 13,290 millimeters of rain every year.

Lloró might be the wettest place, but the coldest is Antarctica. The lowest temperature there is minus 89 degrees Celsius. It is also the driest and windiest place too. There are winds over 300 kilometers per hour all year round. That's about the same speed as a typhoon. Unlike the cold, dry wind of Antarctica, typhoons need warm water and wet air. You can find them in the Philippines. It gets seven or eight on land every year!

Extra Info

City	Yuma, Arizona	Lloró	Manila
Country	The United States	Colombia	The Philippines
Temperature (July)	34.3°C	22.5°C	28.5°C
Temperature (January)	13.6°C	22.2°C	26.5°C
Rain (yearly)	80 mm	13,290 mm	2,201 mm
Wind	13.5 km/h	16 km/h	19 km/h

°C = degrees Celsius mm = millimeter km/h = kilometers per hour

Sources: U.S. National Climatic Data Center, World Meteorological Organization

A. Weather Adjectives

Write the adjectives from the article below the pictures. Use the hints to help you.

1

________ (has the lowest temperature)

2

________ (is a little hot)

3

________ (has the most sun)

4

________ (has the least rain)

5

________ (has the most wind)

6

________ (has the most rain)

B. Fill in the Missing Letters

Complete the sentences with the words from the article.

1. The **s**________ place on earth is in Arizona.
2. Lloró, Colombia, has 13,290 millimeters of **r**________ every year.
3. The lowest **t**________ in Antarctica is minus 89 **d**________ Celsius.
4. Antarctica is the **w**________ place in the world. The wind is really strong.
5. The winds go at a **s**________ of 300 kilometers per hour in Antarctica.
6. The Philippines gets seven or eight **t**________ on land every year.

C. Multiple Choice

Circle the answers.

1. How much sun does Yuma get every day?
   - **a.** 4,050 hours
   - **b.** 50 hours
   - **c.** 11 hours
   - **d.** It's sunny all the time.

2. Which is the driest place in the world?
   - **a.** Yuma, Arizona
   - **b.** Antarctica
   - **c.** The Philippines
   - **d.** All of them

3. Where do typhoons form?
   - **a.** Places with warm water and dry air
   - **b.** Places with cold water and wet air
   - **c.** Places with lots of air and no water
   - **d.** Places with warm water and wet air

4. What is similar between Antarctica and Yuma?
   - **a.** They are both very dry.
   - **b.** They are both really wet.
   - **c.** They both have typhoons.
   - **d.** They are both in the United States.

UNIT
4 The World of Computers

Expressions

Listen and write the correct letters in the blanks. Track 24

ⓐ Yes. I use my computer three hours every day
ⓑ Yes, I have my own computer
ⓒ Yes, I use my computer
ⓓ My computer is fine
ⓔ It doesn't work
ⓕ Yes, I do. It's quicker

Owning a Computer

A: Do you have your own computer?
B: 1. ____________.

Problems

A: Is your computer OK?
B: No. 2. ____________.

Habits

A: Do you use your computer often?
B: 3. ____________.

School Use

A: Do you type up homework on your computer?
B: 4. ____________.

Small Talk *Practice the dialogues above using these expressions.*

Owning a Computer

No. I share a computer with my sister.
No. I use my roommate's computer.

Problems

No. It's very slow.
Not really. I need a new one.

Habits

Yes. I use my computer every day.
No. I don't often use it.

School Use

No. I write my homework by hand.
Yes. I type up some of my homework.

1. What do you usually do on the computer?
2. How much time do you spend on the computer every day?
3. Is your computer important to you? In what way?

Words

Listen and repeat the phrases. **Track 25**

Act It Out

Practice talking about ***functions of computers*** *with a partner.*

Question	Response
What do you use your computer for? What do you do on your computer?	I use it for homework. I use it for games. I often send e-mails. I use my computer to watch videos. I listen to music on my computer. I seldom use it.

Listen Up

Task I *Listen to the three speakers. What do they use computers for?* **Track 26**

Joe	Abby	Abby's Sister
1. ______________	1. ______________	1. ______________
2. ______________		2. ______________
3. ______________		

Task II *Listen again and fill in the blanks with the words you hear.*

1. Joe has a __________ computer.
2. He spends __________ __________ every day on the computer.
3. Abby uses the computer for __________ __________ per day.
4. Abby's sister spends __________ __________ time on it.

Conversation

Save My Computer!

Sara and Ken are in the living room. Track 27

Sara: Hi, Ken. Are you **busy**?[1]

Ken: Hi, Sara. What's up? You look **nervous**.[2]

Sara: There's a problem with my computer. I can't **turn** it **on**,[3] and I need to send an e-mail.

Ken: That doesn't sound good. You can always send your e-mail from my computer or my iPhone.

Sara: I also have to **type up**[4] my homework. I need my computer!

Ken: Well, I'm good with computers. I can take a look.

Sara: Thanks a lot!

(after ten minutes . . .)

Ken: Sorry, it still doesn't **work**.[5] I'm not able to **fix**[6] it. You should take it to a computer **store**.[7]

Sara: That's a good **idea**.[8] Can you come with me? I don't know a lot about computers.

Ken: No problem.

Sara: You are a nice **person**[9] and a great friend!

Role Play

Use the words to make your own conversations.

- watch my sister's son / write a letter / do my math homework
- babies / words / numbers
- love children / am a great writer / am good at math

A: You look nervous.

B: Yes, I am. Can you help me?

A: What's up?

B: I need to ____________. I'm not good with ____________.

A: No problem. I ____________.

B: Thanks a lot!

A. Key Words Track 28

1. **busy** *adj.*
I am very busy. I have a lot of homework.

2. **nervous** *adj.*
Jesse is nervous. He starts his new job today.

3. **turn on** *phr.*
Kathy, can you turn on the TV? I want to watch the news.

4. **type up** *phr.*
I like to write my notes by hand first and then type them up.

5. **work** *v.*
I have to take a taxi. My car doesn't work.

6. **fix** *v.*
This chair is broken. I need to fix it.

7. **store** *n.*
This book is cheaper at the other store.

8. **idea** *n.*
It's a bad idea to go out during the typhoon.

9. **person** *n.*
Jack is the tallest person here. He's almost 200 centimeters tall.

B. Listening Key Track 29

Listen and complete the sentences with the words you hear.

1. Joe looks __________.
2. Joe doesn't have time to relax. He's really __________.
3. Joe has to __________ __________ a report.
4. Joe doesn't want a beer. He has __________ __________ __________work to do.
5. Bryan can't __________ __________ the TV.
6. They need to __________ the TV.

C. Language Tips

1. A Lot vs. A Lot Of

Verb + a lot	a lot of + Noun
I don't know **a lot** about computers.	There are **a lot of** cars on the road.
Thanks **a lot** for your help.	I have **a lot of** friends.
I love my family **a lot**.	Jason doesn't make **a lot of** money.

2. Talking about Problems

There is a problem with my + Noun.	Noun + is broken.
Noun + doesn't work.	I need to fix my + Noun.

Look at the pictures and fill in the blanks.

1. There is a __________ with Eric's phone. It doesn't __________. He can't make any calls.

2. Pam's camera is __________. The pictures are not clear. She needs to __________ it.

Grammar

Coordinating Conjunctions

Coordinating conjunctions join two ideas. Both parts need to be the same (noun and noun, adjective and adjective).

Conjunction	Usage	Example
and	join similar ideas	I can't turn it on, and I need to send an e-mail. (join two clauses) You are a nice person and a great friend! (join two phrases)
but	show different ideas	He is short but strong. (join two adjectives) Olive is very smart, but her sister isn't. (join two clauses)
or	give choices	You can always send your e-mail from my computer or my iPhone. (join two nouns) We can go to the movies or have some dinner. (join two phrases)

Sensing Verbs

We usually use **sensing verbs** in the following two ways.

sensing verb	+ adjective
	+ like + noun

Verb	Example
look	What's up? You look nervous. This city looks like Paris.
feel	Do you feel tired? It is very hot today. It feels like summer.
taste	I often go to the coffee shop. The cakes there taste delicious. This tofu tastes like chicken.
smell	David's shoes smell bad. The inside of the car smells like smoke.
sound	That machine sounds loud. Does it sound like Japanese to you?

A. Fill in the Blanks

*Use the words **and**, **but**, **or** to complete the sentences.*

1. At 4 p.m., I finish work __________ go home.
2. I want a can of Coke, __________ I don't have any money.
3. Would you like to take a bus __________ take a taxi?
4. I don't see him often, __________ I talk to him on the phone every day.
5. I want to listen to some music __________ relax.
6. Is the post office on Parnell Street, __________ is it on O'Connell Street?
7. I like my brother, __________ I like my sister more.
8. Can you sing __________ play the piano at the same time?

B. Match

Match the two parts.

1. He doesn't look like •	• and the service is good too.
2. This tastes like a potato, •	• but he is actually from England.
3. The speaker sounds Australian, •	• and flowers in the garden.
4. The cheese smells like dirty socks, •	• but I'm not ready for it.
5. That restaurant's food tastes delicious, •	• or I can go to yours.
6. You can come to my house, •	• a student or a teacher.
7. There are a lot of trees •	• but it tastes great.
8. The exam is today, •	• but it's really a pumpkin.

C. Complete the Passage

Use the word choices given to complete the passage.

and	looks	tastes	and	smells	or	but	and	or	wonderful

The pie is easy to make! You need cheese, bacon, **1.** __________ eggs. First, mix six eggs in one bowl. Then, you put the bacon **2.** __________ cheese in another bowl. Next, you add the eggs, onions, **3.** __________ some cream. You can also use a little salt **4.** __________ pepper. Bake it in the oven for 40 **5.** __________ 50 minutes. It's ready when it **6.** __________ golden and **7.** __________ delicious. A cold pie is good, **8.** __________ a hot one **9.** __________ even better. They both sound **10.** __________ when you are hungry!

Reading

Before You Read

Look at the pictures. What are these tools for? What do you think the reading is about?

The Internet in Your Pocket

Track 30

While You Read

1. What is the Mobile Internet?

2. What can we use it for?

3. How are smartphones better than computers for the Internet?

Do you prefer to surf the Internet on your PC or on your phone? Almost everybody has a smartphone, and today more and more people use their phones to access the Internet. This is called the Mobile Internet. Most people use it to check e-mails, play games, or use Facebook. They do not need to be at home or at work to use the Mobile Internet. People can surf the Internet from a bus or a train. According to the eMarketer, more than 1.76 billion people worldwide have a smartphone. A Common Sense Media found that 38% of children under two have used smartphones before they could speak in full sentences.

Extra Info

Look at the use of the Mobile Internet:

Country	Mobile Internet Users
The U.S.	136,600,000
Japan	106,300,000
Korea	38,800,000
Italy	34,300,000
The U.K.	29,500,000

Sources: Google Statistics, Morgan Stanley Research

A. Fill in the Missing Letters

Complete the sentences with the words from the article.

1. Almost everyone owns a **s**__________.
2. Today, many people prefer to use their phones to surf the **I**__________.
3. You can use the Mobile Internet for Facebook, e-mails, and **g**__________.
4. Mobile Internet users don't need to be at **h**__________ or at **w**__________.
5. You can use the Mobile Internet from a bus or a **t**__________.
6. Some **c**__________ can use a smartphone, but they cannot speak in full sentences.

B. True or False

*Check (✓) **True** or **False**.*

	Statement	True	False
1	The Mobile Internet is very popular now.		
2	People only use Facebook on their PC.		
3	Mobile Internet users keep decreasing.		
4	Children get a smartphone after they speak in sentences.		
5	You can use the Mobile Internet on public transportation.		
6	Smartphones are useful for surfing the Internet.		

C. Multiple Choice

Circle the answers.

1. Today more and more people prefer to surf the Internet with a(n) __________.
   - **a.** personal computer
   - **b.** Internet café
   - **c.** smartphone
   - **d.** home phone

2. Where can people use the Mobile Internet?
   - **a.** At home
   - **b.** In the office
   - **c.** On the bus
   - **d.** All of the above

3. Why do people use the Mobile Internet?
   - **a.** They can bring their phones everywhere.
   - **b.** They don't have cameras.
   - **c.** They don't stay at home.
   - **d.** They can't use computers.

4. What can't you do with the Mobile Internet?
   - **a.** Play games
   - **b.** Post on Facebook
   - **c.** Send e-mails
   - **d.** Surf in the ocean

UNIT 5

Man's Best Friends

Expressions

Listen and write the correct letters in the blanks. Track 31

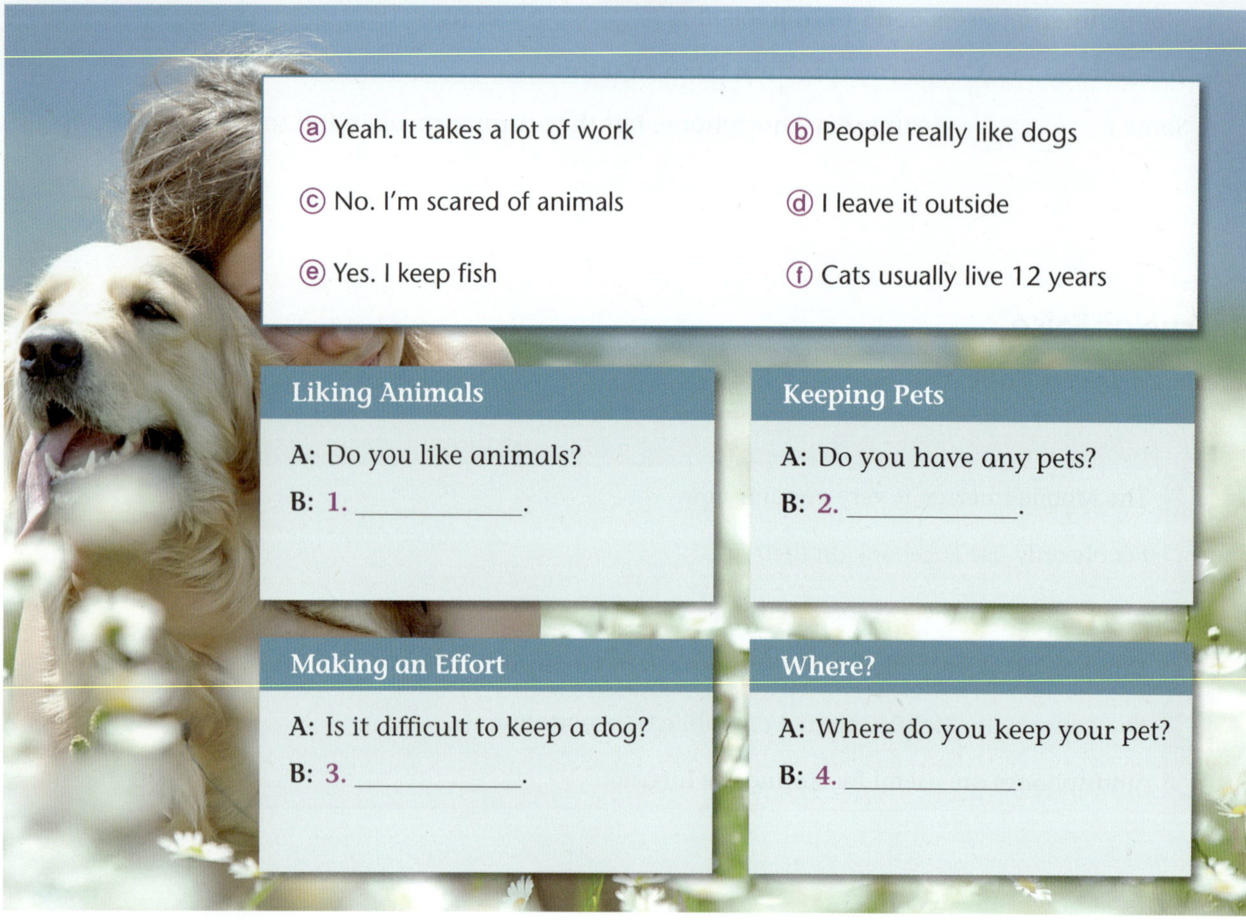

ⓐ Yeah. It takes a lot of work

ⓑ People really like dogs

ⓒ No. I'm scared of animals

ⓓ I leave it outside

ⓔ Yes. I keep fish

ⓕ Cats usually live 12 years

Liking Animals

A: Do you like animals?
B: 1. ____________.

Keeping Pets

A: Do you have any pets?
B: 2. ____________.

Making an Effort

A: Is it difficult to keep a dog?
B: 3. ____________.

Where?

A: Where do you keep your pet?
B: 4. ____________.

Small Talk

Practice the dialogues above using these expressions.

Liking Animals

Yes. I love animals.
No. I don't like animals.
No. I hate animals.

Keeping Pets

Yes. I have a dog.
Sure. We have a cat at home.
No. I don't have any pets.

Making an Effort

Yeah. It's hard work.
Yes. It's not easy.
No. It's easy.
Not really. It's no problem.

Where?

It lives inside.
I keep it in a cage.
My pet lives in the yard.

1. Do you have any pets?
2. What's the best thing about having a pet?
3. Which animal is your favorite? Why?

Words

Listen and repeat the words. Track 32

1 
rabbit *n.*

2 
snake *n.*

3 
kitten *n.*

4 
cat *n.*

5 
puppy *n.*

6 
dog *n.*

7 
fish *n.*

8 
bird *n.*

Act It Out

Practice talking about **pets** *with a partner.*

Question	Response
What can your pet do?	My puppy can jump. My bird can sing.
What do you like doing with your pet?	I like walking my dog. I like to play with my kitten. I like watching my fish.
What is your pet like?	My rabbit is very cute.

Listen Up

Task I *Listen and fill in the blanks with the words you hear.* Track 33

1. Lydia loves ____________.
2. Charles likes to watch his ____________. It makes him feel ____________.
3. His pets are ____________ to ____________.
4. It's hard ____________ keeping cats and dogs, but it can be ____________.

Task II *Listen again and fill in the right name (Charles or Lydia).*

1. My puppy opens the door sometimes.	________
2. I have very quiet pets.	________
3. My pets are smart.	________
4. My cats jump really high.	________

Conversation

The Perfect Pet

Hugh and Penelope are at a pet store. Track 34

Hugh: I need to buy a **toy**[1] for my puppy.

Penelope: Oh, I love puppies. Is it **male**[2] or **female**?[3]

Hugh: It's female. She's eight weeks old.

Penelope: Is she **smart**?[4] You should **train**[5] her.

Hugh: Training a puppy is not an easy job. I enjoy walking her, but she runs away too much.

Penelope: I want to get a pet, but my **apartment**[6] is very small, and I don't have a **yard**.[7]

Hugh: So you can't get an elephant or a **panda**.[8]

Penelope: Ha-ha! No, I can't. Maybe I could keep a snake or some fish.

Hugh: How about a bird? Some birds are really beautiful.

Penelope: I don't like to see birds in **cages**.[9] They can't fly.

Hugh: Then we should look at cats.

Penelope: Good idea.

Role Play *Use the words to make your own conversations.*

Animal		dog	cat	monkey
What's it like?	+ adj.	friendly smart	clean quiet	cute funny
	– adj.	noisy	unfriendly	naughty

A: I want a __________ (+ adj.) pet.
B: You should get a __________.
A: They're too __________ (– adj.).
B: Then you can get a __________.
A: Good idea! They're __________ (+ adj.).

A. Key Words Track 35

1. **toy** *n.* My baby sister loves this doll. It's her favorite toy.	2. **male** *adj.* Male animals are usually bigger.
3. **female** *adj.* Female animals have babies.	4. **smart** *adj.* John is a smart guy. He gets good grades in school.
5. **train** *v.* You can train a cat to use the toilet.	6. **apartment** *n.* I live in a big apartment with three roommates.
7. **yard** *n.* In summer, I often sit in the yard and read a book.	8. **panda** *n.* Pandas are black and white animals. They live in China.
9. **cage** *n.* The monkeys at the zoo are in a cage.	

B. Listening Key Track 36

Listen and complete the sentences with the words you hear.

1. Uncle Bob's job is to __________ animals.
2. He has a __________ elephant and two __________ lions.
3. He keeps the elephant in a big __________.
4. The lions __________ hurt people, so they should stay in a __________.
5. Her uncle __________ pictures of animals to her every month.

C. Language Tips

1. Direct and Indirect Objects

I need to buy a toy for my puppy. → I need to buy my puppy a toy.	They give a gift to Jenny every year. → They give Jenny a gift every year.

Rewrite the sentences.

1. I buy food for my family. ▶ I ____________________.
2. Pass me the salt, please. ▶ Pass ____________________, please.

2. Should vs. Could

Modal	Usage	Example
should	Something is a good idea.	You should train her.
could	Something is a choice.	Maybe I could keep a snake or some fish.

Fill in the blanks with ***should*** *or* ***could****.*

1. You __________ stop smoking. It's bad for you.
2. We __________ go out or stay at home.
3. Harry __________ come home for Christmas. Mom really wants to see him.

Grammar

Gerunds and Infinitives

Form

Gerund	Verb + –ing	working	listening	seeing	reading	going
Infinitive	to...	to work	to listen	to see	to read	to go

Usage

	Function	Example
Gerund	subject	Training a puppy is not an easy job.
	complement	My favorite hobby is reading.
	object	I enjoy walking my dog.
Infinitive	subject	To run often is good for your health.
	complement	His dream is to become an actor.
	object	I prefer to keep animals outside.

Usage Note

1. **Infinitives** as subjects sound formal. Most people use **gerunds**.
   To learn a language is difficult. (less common)
   Learning a language is difficult. (more common)

2. Only **gerunds** can be the object of a preposition.
   He knows a lot about **cooking**.
   ~~He knows a lot about **to cook**.~~

Verbs with Gerunds / Infinitives

Gerund / Infinitive	Verb				Example
Gerund	avoid keep	mind miss	enjoy suggest	finish quit	Why do you **keep** talking? I **miss** seeing my family.
Infinitive	hope promise	learn want	plan need	prefer	He **hopes** to go to Europe next year. They can **learn** to play the guitar.
Gerund or Infinitive	begin love	start	hate	like	Do you **like** playing sports? (Do you **like** to play sports?)

A. Fill in the Blanks

Write the correct form of the words to complete the sentences. For some questions, more than one answer is correct.

1. I hate ___________(see) that guy.
2. When do you plan ___________ (eat) dinner?
3. We always finish ___________ (practice) at 6 o'clock.
4. Marsha loves ___________ (be) the best at everything.
5. ___________ (Go) to the movies on weekends is fun.
6. You can begin ___________ (write) now, class!
7. The most important thing is ___________ (find) a good doctor.
8. June is really good at ___________ (plant) flowers.

B. Correct the Mistakes

Fix the errors in the sentences.

1. I need to finishing a report today. ▸ ___________________________
2. Make bread is not a difficult thing to do. ▸ ___________________________
3. I don't want eating too much food at the party. ▸ ___________________________
4. Justine liking to listen to loud music. ▸ ___________________________
5. I'm sorry for to be late. ▸ ___________________________
6. Andrew enjoys run in the morning. ▸ ___________________________
7. Annie is a hard worker. She doesn't mind to work late. ▸ ___________________________
8. My plan is buy a big house this year. ▸ ___________________________

C. Complete the Passage

Use the correct form of the words in parentheses to complete the passage.

Do you like **1.** ___________ (watch) stars at night? Since it is not easy **2.** ___________ (see) stars in the city, many people enjoy **3.** ___________ (go) to rural areas. People easily can see a bright "star" at night. It is not a star. It is Mars. **4.** ___________ (Fly) to Mars is difficult, but some people dream about **5.** ___________ (move) there. Mars is a cold and dry planet, but some scientists found out some large areas of water there. Mars is the fourth planet from the Sun. Therefore, Mars is a lot colder than earth. The average temperature on Mars is minus 63 degrees Celsius. If we want **6.** ___________ (live) there, we need **7.** ___________ (warm) the planet up. Do you want **8.** ___________ (fly) living there, or do you prefer **9.** ___________ (live) on earth?

Reading

Before You Read

Look at the picture. What do you think the story is about?

Want a Bigger Pet?

Track 37

While You Read

1. What kind of pet does the Joubert family keep?
2. Where do they keep the animal?
3. What can the animal do?

Tonie and Shirley Joubert have a special pet, Jessica. Jessica is a nine-year-old hippo. That's a teenager in human years. The family pet weighs 1,000 kilograms. Tonie and Shirley Joubert treat her like a daughter. Jessica can understand a few words of English. She loves to drink coffee. She can drink 20 liters of coffee a day. She enjoys playing with the family's dog. She even eats his food sometimes. After breakfast, Jessica goes to swim with wild hippos in the river. She can leave the Joubert family any time, but she always comes back for dinner. Jessica spends the night in the yard. Tonie tries to keep her out of the house, but Jessica can open the door. She often breaks furniture in the house. Jessica is usually gentle. But hippos are very dangerous animals. Don't try to keep one in your apartment!

Extra Info

Take a look at other strange pets:

A couple from Kenya keeps eight giraffes.
The giraffes run around their big house.
They often come to the house for breakfast.

Leszek Bielenda is a rich man from Poland.
He keeps a pet lion in his yard.
Sometimes, they sleep in the same bed.

A. Fill in the Missing Letters

Complete the sentences with the words from the article.

1. Jessica is the Joubert family's pet **h**__________.
2. She's like a **d**__________ to Tonie and Shirley Joubert. They **t**__________ her like family.
3. She **u**__________ some English words.
4. She enjoys **d**__________ coffee. She drinks it every day.
5. She swims with **w**__________ hippos in the river after she has **b**__________.
6. She can leave **a**__________ **t**__________, but she is always back for dinner.
7. Tonie leaves Jessica in the **y**__________ at night.
8. Sometimes, Jessica enters the house and breaks **f**__________.

B. Words in Context

Choose the answers.

1. Dylan is a **teenager**. He is young / old.
2. About half of all **humans** live in cities. Animals / People like to live together.
3. I **understand** a little French. I know / ask the meanings of a few words.
4. These **wild** flowers grow in nature / the basement.
5. My son breaks things **a lot**. We often / seldom need to fix them.
6. The store sells **furniture**. You can find some nice T-shirts and pants / tables and chairs there.
7. He's a very **gentle** boy. He always / never fights.
8. That river is **dangerous**. It runs very fast / slow.

C. Find the Facts

Check (✓) the correct box.

☐

Name: Jessica
Age: nine
Weight: one hundred kilograms
Favorite drink: water (20 liters a day)
Sleeps in: the Jouberts' house
She can: swim, open the door, speak English

☐

Name: Jessica
Type: hippo
Favorite drink: coffee
Favorite sport: swimming
Loves: playing with the dog, swimming in the river
She can: understand a little English
Sleeps in: the Jouberts' yard

UNIT 6

At the Department Store

Expressions

Listen and write the correct letters in the blanks. Track 38

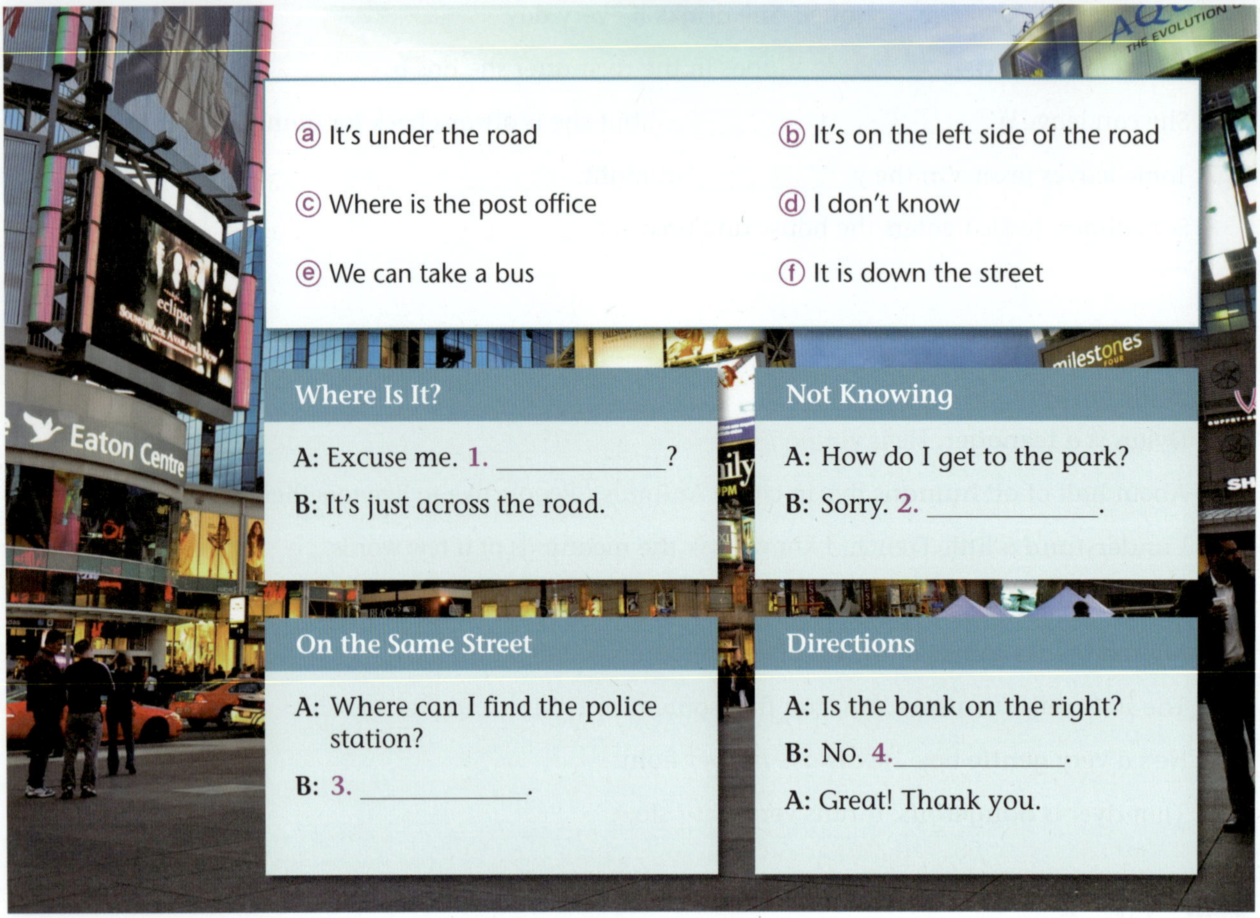

ⓐ It's under the road
ⓑ It's on the left side of the road
ⓒ Where is the post office
ⓓ I don't know
ⓔ We can take a bus
ⓕ It is down the street

Where Is It?

A: Excuse me. 1. ___________?
B: It's just across the road.

Not Knowing

A: How do I get to the park?
B: Sorry. 2. ___________.

On the Same Street

A: Where can I find the police station?
B: 3. ___________.

Directions

A: Is the bank on the right?
B: No. 4. ___________.
A: Great! Thank you.

Small Talk

Practice the dialogues above using these expressions.

Where Is It?

How can I get to the school?
Which direction is the post office in?
How do I get to the supermarket?

Not Knowing

I have no idea. Sorry.
I'm sorry. I'm not from around here.

On the Same Street

Go straight.
Keep walking.
It's two doors down.

Directions

It's on your left.
It's on the right.
It's on the left-hand side.

1. Do you like department stores? Why or why not?
2. What do they sell there?
3. Do you need anything from the department store?

Words

Listen and repeat the words. Track 39

1 stairs *n.*

2 basement *n.*

Photo: adrimcm / Flickr

3 food court *n.*

Photo: rick / Flickr

4 men's department *n.*

5 building *n.*

6 floor *n.*

7 restroom *n.*

8 information desk *n.*

Photo: mikeleeorg / Flickr

Act It Out

*Practice talking about **where things are** with a partner.*

Question	Response
Where is the men's department?	It's on the third floor. It's beside the women's department.
Where are the restrooms?	They're in the basement. They're at the back of the store. They're behind the information desk.
Where is Mark?	He's in front of the building. He's next to the stairs. He's between the food court and the restrooms.

Listen Up

*Listen and check (✓) **True** or **False**.* Track 40

	Statement	True	False
1	They are at the department store now.		
2	It is hard to find the department store.		
3	Bel Air is the department store's name.		
4	Fresh Plaza has a nice men's department.		
5	The food court is on the first floor.		

Conversation

Shopping for Clothes

*Bob and Timmy are in a **department store**.*[1] Track 41

Bob: Wow! There are a lot of people here.

Timmy: Yeah, there are. I need a **baseball cap**.[2] Where are they?

Bob: Um, I don't know. Ask the **clerk**.[3] She's near the door.

Timmy: I'm sorry. Where are the baseball caps?

Clerk: They're on the second floor. We're in the basement now.

Timmy: Where are the stairs?

Clerk: First, go **straight**.[4] Turn right at the food court and walk **toward**[5] the T-shirts. The stairs are on the left.

Timmy: Great! Thanks.

Clerk: No problem.

Bob: Come on.

(*They walk **upstairs**.*[6])

Timmy: I can't see them!

Bob: Look over there. They are near the **gloves**,[7] on the right.

Timmy: Oh, here they are. This one is cool.
Let's go to the food court after I buy it.

Bob: Wonderful! Where's the food court?

Timmy: Oh man! You're **terrible**[8] with **directions**.[9]

Role Play

Use the map to make your own conversations.

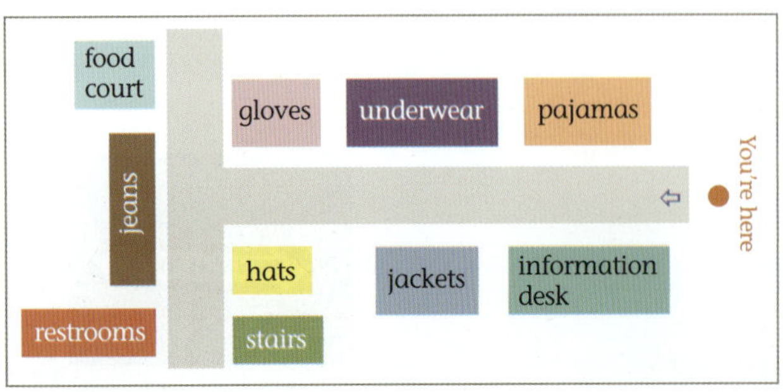

A: Excuse me, where is/are the ___________?

B: Walk straight. Go past the ___________.
(Turn ___________.) It's/They're on the ___________.

A: Thank you.

B: You're welcome.

A. Key Words Track 42

1. **department store** *n.* Harrods is a famous department store in London.	2. **baseball cap** *n.* A baseball cap can keep the sun out of your eyes.
3. **clerk** *n.* Betsy is a clerk in a shoe store.	4. **straight** *adv.* Go straight down the street. The hospital is on the left.
5. **toward** *prep.* My house is over there toward the park.	6. **upstairs** *adv.* The house has two bedrooms upstairs.
7. **glove** *n.* (usually plural) Ted's hands get very cold. He wears gloves in winter.	8. **terrible** *adj.* Lisa is not a good cook. Her food always tastes terrible.
9. **direction** *n.* The sea is in that direction. You can walk there in five minutes.	

B. Listening Key Track 43

Listen and complete the sentences with the words you hear.

1. Dan wants to know the ____________ of the store.
2. Dan has to go ____________ toward the hospital. Then, turn ____________ on Shannon Road.
3. Roseanne is a ____________ in a department store.
4. The store sells ____________ and caps.
5. Dan stops the car on the ____________.

C. Language Tips

1. Left and Right

*We can use **left** and **right** in different places in a sentence.*

The stairs are on the **left**. — Noun
Turn **right** at the food court. — Adverb
The library is on the **left** side. — Adjective

Check (✓) the correct part of speech.

1. I use my **right** hand when eating food.	☐ Noun	☐ Adverb	☐ Adjective
2. You need to turn **left** after the post office.	☐ Noun	☐ Adverb	☐ Adjective
3. At the light, take a **right**.	☐ Noun	☐ Adverb	☐ Adjective

2. Showing Emotions

Expression	Meaning
Wow! There are a lot of people here.	I'm surprised.
Um, I don't know.	I'm not sure.
Oh man! You're terrible with directions.	That's bad.

Grammar

Imperatives

Forms

Type	Structure	Example
Positive	Base form of the verb.	Ask the clerk.
Negative	Do not + base form.	Don't eat all the cake.
With Name	Base form, (*name*).	Sit down, Mike.
	Do not + base form, (*name*).	Don't make me angry, Bruce.
Polite	(Do not) + base form, please. Please + (do not) + base form.	Close the door, please. Please don't make any noise.
Strong	Do + base form.	Do call me when you get there.
	Never + base form.	Never run with a knife.

Usage Note

An imperative sentence usually doesn't have its subject: **you**.

Functions

Usage	Example
Instructions	Walk straight.
Orders	Don't run away, Kevin.
Offers	Try the pizza. It's pretty good.
Invitations	Come over to our house. We have lots of food.
Advice	Drink more water and get some sleep.
Warnings	Watch out! There's a car behind you!

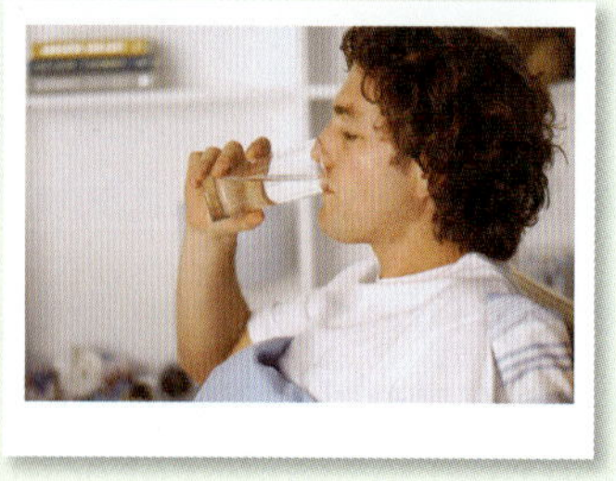

The Imperative with *Let's*

Let's means **Let us.** The speaker asks the listener to do something together.

Type	Structure	Example
Positive	Let's + base form.	Let's go to the food court after I finish my work.
Negative	Let's + not + base form.	Let's not go out tonight.

A. Put in Order

Put the words in the correct order.

1. road. / Don't / the / cross ▸ ______________________
2. you. / your / Keep / bag / with ▸ ______________________
3. and / the / straight. / right / first / Take / drive ▸ ______________________
4. tea / with / afternoon. / some / Have / us / this ▸ ______________________
5. house. / back / the / to / go / Let's ▸ ______________________
6. relax. / Please / in / come / and ▸ ______________________
7. The / red. / light / is / careful! / Be ▸ ______________________
8. of / Try / cookies. / our / some / famous ▸ ______________________

B. Match

Match the sentences.

_____	**1.** Never stand in the road.	**a.** I didn't hear you.
_____	**2.** Do visit us in New York.	**b.** It's rude.
_____	**3.** Come over here and look at this picture.	**c.** I need to call Carlos.
_____	**4.** Please say it again.	**d.** It is very cold today.
_____	**5.** Don't tell Bob about this.	**e.** I don't want him to know about this.
_____	**6.** Please give me the phone.	**f.** We can go for dinner together.
_____	**7.** Don't talk to me like that.	**g.** It's dangerous.
_____	**8.** Close the window, Alex.	**h.** It's a beautiful picture.

C. Complete the Passage

Use the word choices given to complete the passage.

don't put	get	use	make	give	write	put	start	pack	don't mix

How to Pack for Moving

1. __________ yourself a lot of time. __________ weeks before you move.
2. __________ strong boxes. __________ them from a supermarket.
3. __________ one room at a time.
4. __________ things from different rooms in the same box.
5. __________ heavy things at the bottom of the box.
6. __________ the name of the room on the box.
7. __________ a list for each box and the things in it.
8. __________ more than 25 kilograms in a box. Light boxes are easier to carry.

Reading

Before You Read

Look at the pictures. Where do you like to shop? What do you think the reading is about?

A New World of Shopping

Track 44

Do you like shopping? If you do, Shinsegae is a perfect place for you. Shinsegae, the biggest department store in the world, is in South Korea. The name means "new world" in Korean. It is in Centum City in Busan. The store is 14 stories tall. The space is enough to fit 2,300 houses! That's bigger than Macy's in New York. More than 6,000 people work at Shinsegae. It has books, clothes, toys, and a lot more. You can even ice-skate there or play golf on the golf course!

There's a large roof garden too. It also has a new type of restaurant. Cine de Chef serves great food and shows the newest movies. It's easy to get there. You can take the subway in Busan or the train from Seoul to get to Centum City.

While You Read

1. What's the biggest department store?

2. How tall is Shinsegae?

3. How many people work in Shinsegae?

Extra Info

Buying Health

Shopping is fun, but is it good for your health? A new study says *yes*. Shopping helps you to . . .

☑ meet more people. ☑ get more exercise.

☑ think more. ☑ live longer.

A. Fill in the Missing Letters

Complete the sentences with the words from the article.

1. Shinsegae is the world's biggest **d**__________ **s**__________.
2. The building is very high. It has 14 **s**__________.
3. The place is big enough to **f**__________ 2,300 houses.
4. You can play golf on its golf **c**__________.
5. The store sells everything from **c**__________ to books and **t**__________.
6. Cine de Chef is a new type of **r**__________. It **s**__________ delicious food and shows **m**__________.

B. Check for Details

What can you do at Shinsegae?

	Things to Do	Check (✓)
1	See a movie	
2	Have dinner at a nice restaurant	
3	Go fishing with friends	
4	Skate on ice	
5	Build a lot of houses	
6	Play golf	
7	Sit in the roof garden	
8	Look for your favorite books	

Photo: daryl_mitchell / Flickr

C. Fill in the Blanks

Use the correct form of the word choices given to complete the sentences.

mean	serve	clothes	space	ice-skate	type	shop	subway

1. I like to __________ in the market. Things are cheaper there.
2. The restaurant __________ the best spaghetti in town.
3. The new movie theater is really big. There is __________ for 2,000 seats.
4. Red roses are popular on Valentine's Day. They __________ true love.
5. The lake turns into ice in winter. It's fun to __________ on it.
6. Tiffany wears her sister's __________ sometimes.
7. Jazz is Ken's favorite __________ of music.
8. I usually take the __________ to work.

UNIT 7

Daily Life

1. When do you get up?
2. What do you do every day?
3. Do you do housework? How much time do you spend doing it?

Expressions

Listen and write the correct letters in the blanks. Track 45

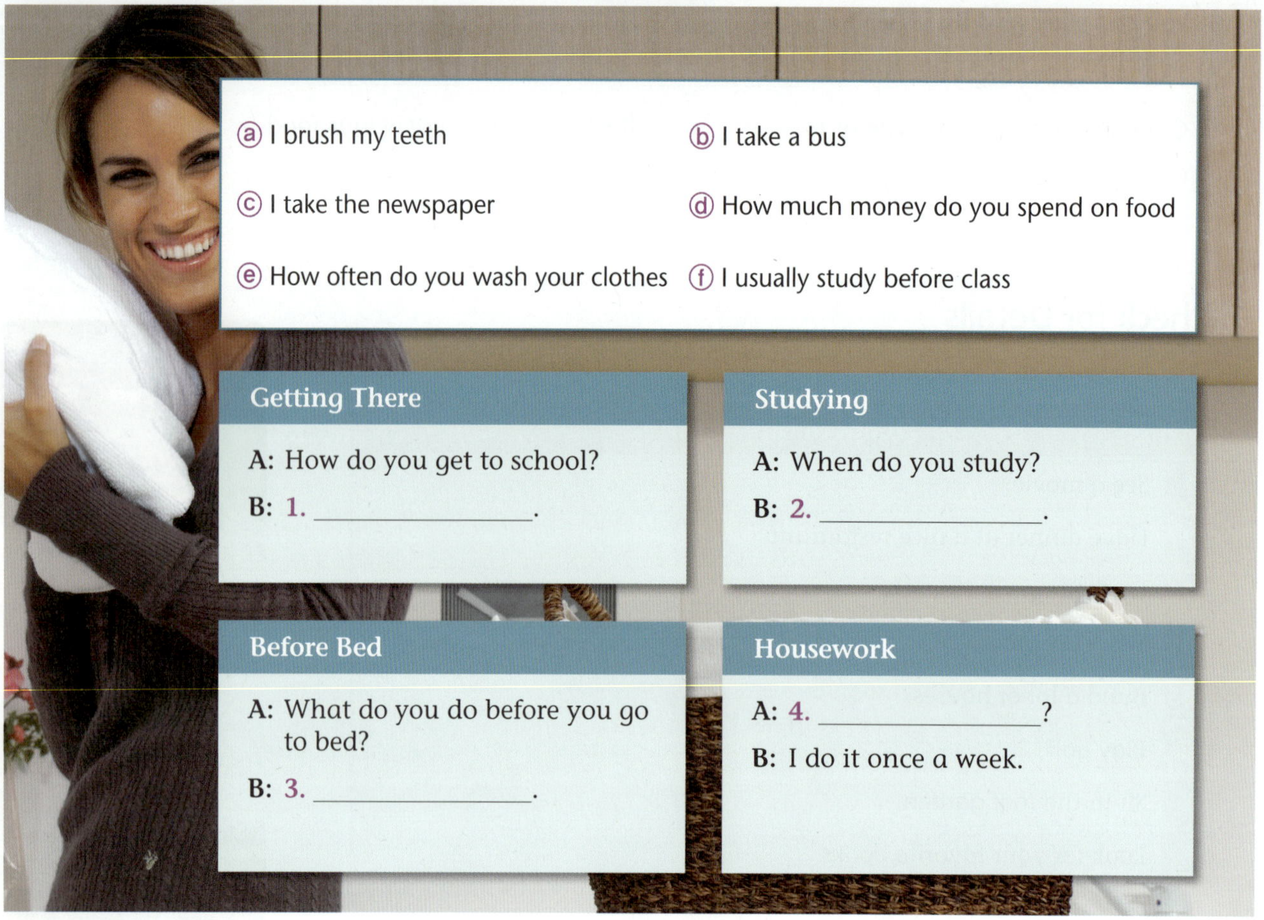

ⓐ I brush my teeth

ⓑ I take a bus

ⓒ I take the newspaper

ⓓ How much money do you spend on food

ⓔ How often do you wash your clothes

ⓕ I usually study before class

Getting There

A: How do you get to school?

B: 1. ________________.

Studying

A: When do you study?

B: 2. ________________.

Before Bed

A: What do you do before you go to bed?

B: 3. ________________.

Housework

A: 4. ________________?

B: I do it once a week.

Small Talk

Practice the dialogues above using these expressions.

Getting There

I ride a scooter.
I walk.
I live in a dorm.

Studying

I like to study at night.
I only study before exams.
I study between classes.

Before Bed

I feed my dog.
I take a shower.
I watch the news.
I read a book.

Housework

When do you clean your apartment?
When do you mop the floor?
How often do you take out the trash?

Words

Listen and repeat the words. **Track 46**

1 **library** *n.*

2 **garage** *n.*

3 **post office** *n.*

4 **dry cleaners** *n.*

5 **ATM** *n.*

6 **gas station** *n.*

7 **hospital** *n.*

8 **drugstore** *n.*

Act It Out

*Practice talking about **places and activities** with a partner.*

Question	Response
Where are you?	I'm at the ATM. I need some money. I'm in the hospital. I don't feel well. I'm in the library. I need to write a report. I'm at the dry cleaners. My jacket is dirty.
Are you busy?	Yes. I need to run to the post office and send a letter. Yes. I have to take my scooter to the garage.

Listen Up

Task I *Listen and complete Jason's schedule.* **Track 47**

dry cleaners
movies
post office
library
fix

10 a.m.	Take the book back to the **1.** ___________
1 p.m.	Get stamps from the **2.** ___________
2 p.m.	**3.** ___________ the scooter
4 p.m.	Take the jacket to the **4.** ___________
8 p.m.	Go to the **5.** ___________ with Melanie

Task II *Listen again and fill in the blanks with the words you hear.*

1. Jason is very ___________ today.

2. The ___________ on his scooter is ___________. He needs to go to the ___________.

3. Melanie wants to meet him after he goes to the ___________ ___________.

4. He needs to have some ___________ on Friday night.

Conversation

Help!

Tom calls Debby on the phone. Track 48

Tom: Hi, Debby. What are you doing?

Debby: Hi, Tom. I'm **doing the dishes**[1] and listening to a radio **show**.[2] How about you?

Tom: I'm walking to school right now. Listen, can you help me?

Debby: Sure. What do you need?

Tom: My brother is at home **alone**.[3] Can you **watch**[4] him? I have class **until**[5] four, and then I have to **pick up**[6] my shirts from the dry cleaners.

Debby: Where are your parents?

Tom: They're **traveling**.[7] There isn't **anyone**[8] in the house.

Debby: I'm almost **finished**[9] doing the dishes. I can go over there in about ten minutes.

Tom: Great! Can you stay until five?

Debby: Yeah, that's fine. I need to buy some medicine at the drugstore, but I can do that after five.

Tom: Thanks, Debby!

Debby: Anytime.

Role Play

Use the words to make your own conversations.

Place	Action
gas station	put gas in my car
library	borrow a book
hospital	visit a sick friend
ATM	get money
dry cleaners	clean my clothes
post office	send a package

A: Where are you going?

B: I'm going to the ____________ (place) to ____________ (action). How about you?

A: I'm going to the ____________ (place). I need to ____________ (action).

B: Maybe we can meet for lunch.

A: OK. See you later!

A. Key Words Track 49

1. **do the dishes** *phr.* I like to cook, but I hate doing the dishes.	2. **show** *n.* My favorite TV show is *The Simpsons.*
3. **alone** *adv.* I don't have any roommates. I live alone.	4. **watch** *v.* I watch Sam's dog when he is not in town.
5. **until** *prep.* I can't go shopping until next week. I don't have any money.	6. **pick up** *phr.* I need to pick my friend up from his house later.
7. **travel** *v.* I like traveling by airplane. The train is too slow.	8. **anyone** *pron.* Does anyone want some food?
9. **finished** *adj.* Are you finished eating dinner? We have to go.	

B. Listening Key Track 50

Listen and complete the sentences with the words you hear.

1. Fabio wants Jessica to ___________ him a ___________.
2. He asks her to ___________ ___________ some bread from the ___________. It is open ___________ 9 p.m.
3. He also needs her to help him ___________ the ___________. He doesn't like doing them ___________.
4. Jessica is almost ___________ studying. She is ___________ to ___________.

C. Language Tips

1. Asking for Help

Question	Response	
Can you help me? Can you do me a favor? Can you give me a hand?	Sure. No problem.	What do you need? What is it? How can I help you?

*Use the following problems to practice **asking for help.***

Can I borrow . . .	Can you help me with . . .
a pen? $20?	my homework? my report?

2. Thanking and Responding

Giving Thanks		Responding	
		Formal	Informal
Thanks Thank you Thanks a lot	(for + Noun).	You are welcome. I'm happy to help.	Anytime. No problem.

A: Thank you for all your help, doctor.

B: No problem.

Grammar

Present Continuous

Statements

Subject	Be Verb	(Not)	Present Participle (Verb + –ing)
I	am	(not)	walking to school right now.
You	are	(not)	writing a letter.
He / She / It	is	(not)	running in the park.
We / You / They	are	(not)	traveling.

Yes / No Questions

Question			Response (+)		Response (–)	
Am	I	talking too loudly?	Yes,	you are.	No,	you aren't.
Are	You	exercising?		I am.		I'm not.
Is	he / she / it	helping you?		he / she / it is.		he / she / it isn't.
Are	we / you / they	driving to New York?		you / we / they are.		you / we / they aren't.

Wh– Questions

Question	Response
What are you doing?	I'm doing the dishes and listening to a radio show.
Where is Jack going?	He's going to work.
Why is your mother shouting?	She's really angry at me.
Who is talking to Samantha?	Henry is talking to Samantha.

Be + Verb + –ing

	Verb Ending	Spelling	Example
Regular	one vowel + one consonant	repeat the consonant, add **–ing**	jog → jogging swim → swimming
	one vowel + one consonant + **–e**	drop **–e**, add **–ing**	come → coming leave → leaving
	others	add **–ing**	eat → eating talk → talking
Irregular	lie → lying die → dying		

A. Make Sentences

*Use the words to make sentences in the **present continuous tense**.*

1. Marcia / look for / her bag ▶ ______________________.
2. it / snow / today ▶ ______________________.
3. my parents / shop / in the department store ▶ ______________________.
4. they / carry / the boxes ▶ ______________________?
5. the man / run / very fast ▶ ______________________.
6. Gina / bake / a cake ▶ ______________________.
7. Dan and his brother / wait / for the bus ▶ ______________________?
8. he / lie / to me ▶ ______________________.

B. Words in Context

Circle the answers.

1. The restaurant is very good. I eat / am eating there every day.
2. Look! Jenny's dogs run / are running down the street.
3. Kate reads / is reading a book now.
4. They sleep / are sleeping in that room every night.
5. Lots of people take / are taking a subway to work.
6. I want to use the bathroom, but Halley takes / is taking a shower.
7. Leonard helps / is helping Janet with French now.
8. I can't talk / be talking right now. I work / am working.

C. Complete the Dialogues

Complete the dialogues.

1	A: What ________ Eric ________ (do)? B: He ________ ________ (play) the drums in his room.	2	A: Where ________ Tony ________ (go)? B: He ________ ________ (go) to a party.
3	A: My brother ________ ________ (write) a book about Africa. B: Great. We ________ (want) to read it.	4	A: Why ________ you ________ (eat) so fast? B: My girlfriend ________ ________ (wait) for me to pick her up.
5	A: ________ you ________ (enjoy) the meal? B: Yes. It's delicious.	6	A: ________ you ________ (listen) to me? B: I ________ ________ (try), but the music is really loud.
7	A: Why ________ Tom ________ (wear) a suit? B: He ________ ________ (go) to an interview.	8	A: What is that noise? ________ the baby ________ (cry)? B: Yeah. It's past her dinnertime. She must be very hungry.

Before You Read

Look at the pictures. Who are these people? What do they do?

Everyday Training of an Astronaut

Track 51

Do you want to work in space? It's not easy. You need a lot of training. The first step is to take basic training. This is 18 months of studying and practicing. The students in NASA have classes every day. They study science, engineering, Russian, and English every day. They learn how to fly airplanes. They need to fly 15 hours each week. They also learn about the space station's computers, radios, and engines. Most importantly, they need to pass a swimming test in the first month. They have to swim 75 meters with their clothes and shoes on. A lot of training is under the water in the NBL(Neutral Buoyancy Laboratory). The NBL is a 22,000,000-liter pool. Walking there feels just like walking in space. You have to swim to fly to space!

While You Read

1. How long does basic training take?

2. What classes do the students take?

3. What kind of swimming test do they have to pass?

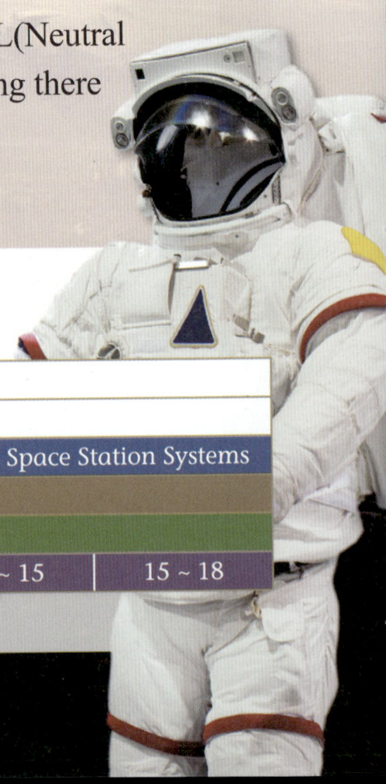

Extra Info

Basic Training Timeline

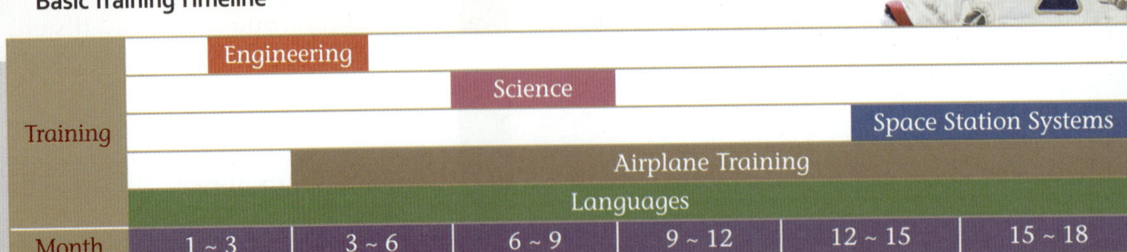

A. Fill in the Missing Letters

Complete the sentences with the words from the article.

1. You need to take **b**__________ training to work in **s**__________.
2. The students have to spend a lot of time **s**__________ and **p**__________.
3. They learn **s**__________, engineering, Russian, and **E**__________.
4. The students learn how to fly **a**__________.
5. They have to fly quite a few **h**__________ each week.
6. The students need to know about the space station's **e**__________, radios, and **c**__________.
7. The **s**__________ test is difficult. They do it with their shoes and **c**__________ on.

B. Fill in the Blanks

Use the word choices given to complete the sentences.

meters	18	hours	75	15	liters	22,000,000	months

1. The students train for __________ __________.
2. Each week, the students fly for __________ __________.
3. During the test, they swim __________ __________.
4. The NBL has __________ __________ of water.

C. True or False

*Check (✓) **True** or **False**.*

	Statement	True	False
1	It takes more than two years to finish basic training.		
2	The basic training is all in space.		
3	The students have language classes every day.		
4	Flying an airplane is part of basic training.		
5	There are engines in the space station.		

D. Find the Facts

Check (✓) the correct box. Which of these schedules would the students have?

☐

8 a.m.	Russian class
10 a.m.	Study science
1 p.m.	Swimming
3 p.m.	Computer systems class
6 p.m.	Flight training

☐

08:00	Swimming test
10:00	Study history
13:00	Watch airplanes
15:00	Play computer games
18:00	English class

UNIT
8 Out in Nature

1. What do you like best about nature?
2. Do you prefer to live in a big city or in a small town?
3. What does your country look like?

Expressions

Listen and write the correct letters in the blanks. Track 52

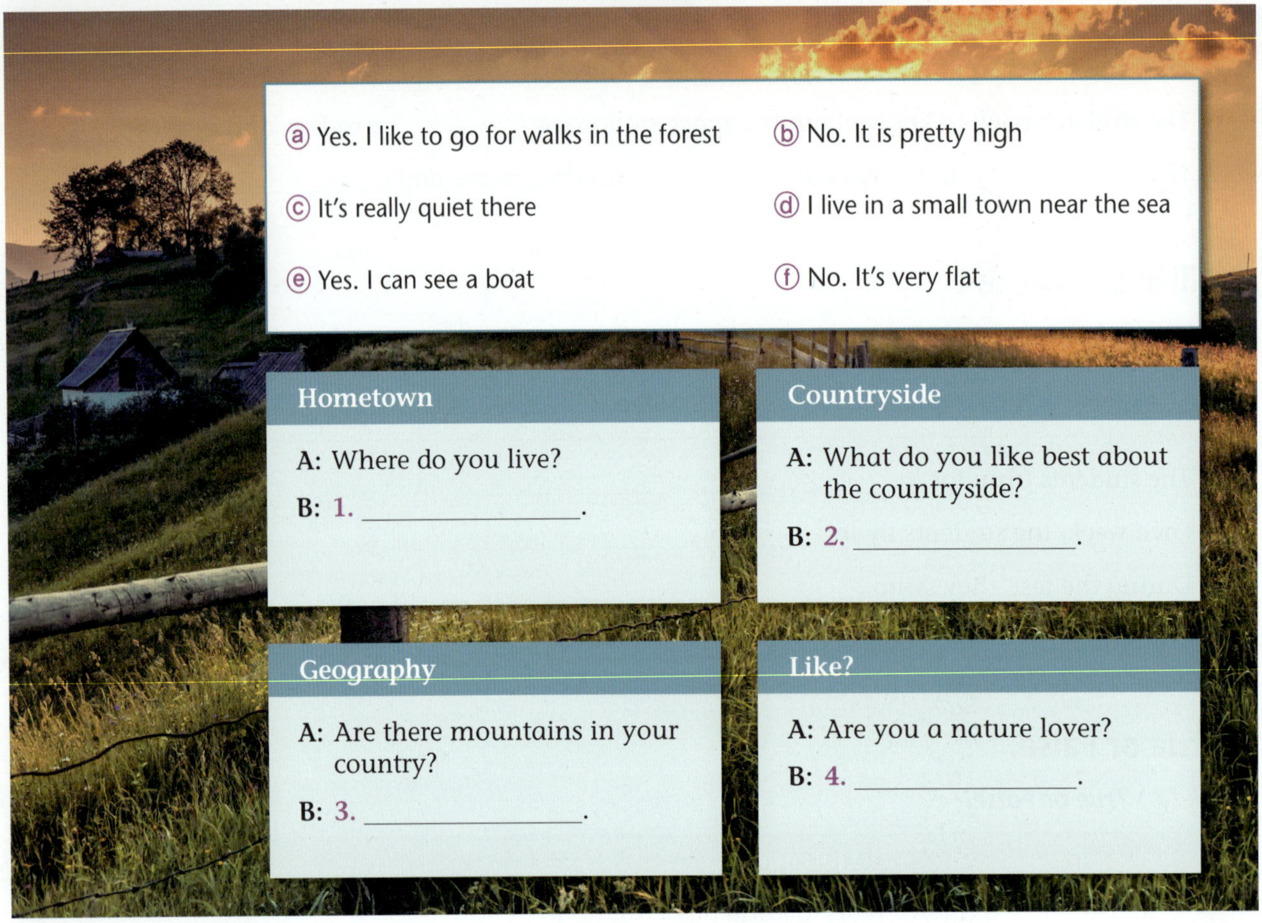

ⓐ Yes. I like to go for walks in the forest
ⓑ No. It is pretty high
ⓒ It's really quiet there
ⓓ I live in a small town near the sea
ⓔ Yes. I can see a boat
ⓕ No. It's very flat

Hometown

A: Where do you live?
B: 1. ________________.

Countryside

A: What do you like best about the countryside?
B: 2. ________________.

Geography

A: Are there mountains in your country?
B: 3. ________________.

Like?

A: Are you a nature lover?
B: 4. ________________.

Small Talk

Practice the dialogues above using these expressions.

Hometown

My hometown is near the forest.
I live on a big farm.
My house is up in the mountains.

Countryside

I enjoy listening to the birds.
The fresh air feels good.
I don't like the countryside. It's boring.

Geography

Yes. There are many mountains.
No. We have a few hills.
Yes. I often go hiking there.

Like?

Yes. It's my favorite thing.
Of course! I love getting away from the city.
No. I'm a city girl.

Words

Listen and repeat the words. Track 53

1

field *n.*

2

forest *n.*

3

beach *n.*

4

lake *n.*

5

island *n.*

6

waterfall *n.*

7

ocean *n.*

8

valley *n.*

Act It Out

*Practice talking about **nature** with a partner.*

Question	Response
What is the countryside like in your country?	There are lots of rice fields. The valleys are very green.
What do you like to do in the open air?	I like to camp in the forest. I love to fish in the ocean. Swimming near the waterfall is the best.
Do you often go to the beach?	Of course. I live on an island. Not often, but there is a lake near my house.

Listen Up

Task I *Listen and match the sentence parts.* Track 54

Where are you •	• or walk through green fields.
What can you •	• in the forest.
You can swim in a lake •	• going?
Also, there is a small waterfall •	• do in the countryside?

Task II *Listen again and fill in the right name (Cal or Rudy).*

1. ____________ likes spending time in the countryside.
2. ____________ prefers TV to nature.
3. ____________ doesn't need TV or Internet.
4. ____________ plans to go camping and look at the stars.
5. ____________ enjoys city life.

Conversation

Nature Walk

Karen and Philip are taking their bags off the train. Track 55

Karen: Where's my map? I want to find it before we **leave**[1] the station.

Philip: You don't need it while I'm here, Karen.

Karen: I do. This is my first time in this **area**.[2]

Philip: I know my way around.

Karen: Oh yeah? What's the **countryside**[3] like around here?

Philip: It's hard to **describe**.[4] You can see when we get out of the city. There are **huge**[5] forests and lots of green fields.

Karen: Are there lakes or beaches?

Philip: There are no beaches, but there are a few small lakes and some waterfalls.

Karen: I can't wait to see them all.

Philip: There are many **colorful**[6] flowers there. It's really **peaceful**.[7]

Karen: Is there a lot of **pollution**?[8]

Philip: It's not a big problem because most people around this area **respect**[9] nature.

Karen: That's great. Ah! Here's my map. Let's go!

Role Play

Use the words to make your own conversations.

Place	Beach	Forest
Activity	swim in the ocean	have a quiet lunch
+ Adj.	fun	peaceful
– Adj.	windy	hot

A: I want to go to a ____________ (+ adj.) place.

B: Why don't you go to the ____________? You can ____________ there.

A: It's too ____________ (– adj.) today.

B: How about the ____________ then? It's ____________ (+ adj.), and you can ____________.

A: Good idea!

A. Key Words Track 56

1. **leave** *v.* The train leaves at 10:30.	2. **area** *n.* There are many good restaurants in this area.
3. **countryside** *n.* I never travel to the countryside. I prefer to stay in the city.	4. **describe** *v.* Describe your country. What is it like?
5. **huge** *adj.* The birthday cake is huge. It's big enough for 20 people.	6. **colorful** *adj.* I like to wear colorful clothes. Bright colors are pretty.
7. **peaceful** *adj.* There are no people or cars here. It is very peaceful.	8. **pollution** *n.* Pollution is a big problem in the city. The air is bad.
9. **respect** *v.* I respect doctors and teachers. They help many people.	

B. Listening Key Track 57

Listen and complete the sentences with the words you hear.

1. The place is very quiet and ____________.
2. Ted asks Adam to ____________ the fish in the ____________. He wants to know what they are ____________.
3. Ted ____________ ____________ to start fishing.
4. The first fish is ____________, and the second fish is ____________.

C. Language Tips

1. The Usage of *Like*

Preposition	What's the countryside like around here?
Verb	Do you like oranges?

Match the question to the answer.

What's he **like**? •	• He likes to play tennis.
What's the weather **like** here? •	• He's a very smart guy.
What does he **like** to do? •	• It's really cold in the winter.

2. Expecting Something Good

Sentence Structure	Example
can't wait (to...)	I can't wait to see them all. This is a nice car. I can't wait to buy it.
be looking forward to + Verb + -ing	I'm looking forward to seeing them all. This is a nice car. I'm looking forward to buying it.

Grammar

Subordinating Conjunctions

Time	
after	We can rest after we finish work.
before	I want to find the map before we leave the station.
while	You don't need the map while I'm here.
when	You can see when we get out of the city.
until	We have two hours until the train comes.

Cause	
because	It's not a big problem because most people around this area respect nature.

Difference	
although / though	Although he is a good student, he doesn't like to study. (Though he is a good student, he doesn't like to study.)

Usage Note

1. Pay attention to the use of the comma (,):
   I like to have coffee **after** I get up.
   (**After** I get up, I like to have coffee.)
   I have two jobs **because** I want to make more money.
   (**Because** I want to make more money, I have two jobs.)

2. Some words have different uses. Compare the examples below:

Part of Speech	Example
subordinating conjunction + Subject + Verb	There is time to eat **before** the movie starts. (*Subject + Verb*) Mary always watches TV **after** she finishes school. (*Subject + Verb*)
preposition + Noun	I go to the gym **before** school every day. (*Noun*) Terry likes to have tea **after** lunch. (*Noun*)

A. Make Sentences

Use the words given to combine the sentences.

1. I am not good at math. / I like it. (although)
   ▸ Although I am ______________________________.
2. It is very clean. / Mary washes the floor. (until)
   ▸ Mary ______________________________.
3. You eat. / You shouldn't do exercise. (after)
   ▸ You shouldn't ______________________________.
4. My sister often buys lots of fruit. / She goes to the market. (when)
   ▸ My sister ______________________________.
5. I like John. / He's a nice guy. (because)
   ▸ I ______________________________.

B. Match

Match the two parts.

1. I listen to music in my room •	• he runs really fast.
2. Don't talk on the phone •	• after she finishes her homework.
3. Dave wants to buy some wine •	• until the class starts.
4. Let's sit here •	• because he is rich.
5. Although Joe is a little fat, •	• before I go to sleep.
6. Julia goes on Facebook •	• when you drive.
7. Mark has a nice car •	• while he is in France.

C. Complete the Passage

Use the word choices given to complete the passage. For some questions, more than one answer is correct.

after	because	until	when	while	before

I work in a zoo **1.** __________ I love animals. I really like working there, but it's not an easy job. My day starts pretty early. It's still dark outside **2.** __________ I get to work. I have to clean the cages **3.** __________ the zoo opens. I eat breakfast **4.** __________ I finish cleaning. Then, I have some free time **5.** __________ I have to feed the animals. It can be dangerous **6.** __________ the lions and tigers are very hungry. People like to watch the snakes **7.** __________ I feed them.

Reading

Before You Read

Look at the pictures. Do you want to visit these places? What do you think the reading is about?

Wonders of the World

Track 58

While You Read

1. What do the three places all have in common?

2. Which one has pollution problems?

3. Where is Lake Baikal?

What are the most interesting places to visit in the world? Here are three beautiful places.

Victoria Falls is between Zambia and Zimbabwe in Africa. It is the biggest waterfall in the world. It is 108 meters high. It's best to see it from the sky. You can swim near the waterfall although it can be dangerous.

The Nile is the longest river in the world. It passes through Egypt. It has two main tributaries: the White Nile and the Blue Nile. Many millions of people in Africa depend on this huge river. It is very famous in history and stories.

Lake Baikal in Russia is the world's biggest and deepest freshwater lake. It's the oldest one too – it's almost 25 million years old. Although pollution in the area is quite serious, the lake is still a beautiful and peaceful place. Be sure to visit it soon before it gets too dirty.

Extra Info

	Victoria Falls	The Nile	Lake Baikal
Best Time to Visit	in May and June	in February and March	from June to August
Things to Do	- riding horses - watching animals	- visiting the pyramids - sailing	- camping - fishing

A. Fill in the Missing Letters

Complete the sentences with the words from the article.

1. The biggest **w**__________ in the world is 108 meters high.
2. Though Victoria Falls is **d**__________, you can **s**__________ in the water.
3. The world's longest **r**__________ has two main **t**__________: the White Nile and the Blue Nile.
4. A lot of people in Africa **d**__________ on the Nile.
5. Lake Baikal is the **o**__________ lake, and it is also the biggest and **d**__________ freshwater lake in the world.
6. Although the area around the lake has **s**__________ **p**__________ problems, it's a **p**__________ place to visit.

B. Classification

Match the statement with the place. Check (✓) the correct boxes.

	Statement	Victoria Falls	The Nile	Lake Baikal
1	It's around 25,000,000 years old.			
2	Many people need it to live.			
3	The place is quiet and makes people feel calm.			
4	It sits between Zambia and Zimbabwe.			
5	Lots of people tell stories about it.			
6	You can enjoy a great view of this from the sky.			

C. Multiple Choice

Circle the answers.

1. What is the passage about?
   - **a.** Horrible accident in Russia
   - **b.** Interesting facts about Egypt
   - **c.** Amazing places on earth
   - **d.** Exciting adventures around the world

2. What are the two tributaries of the Nile?
   - **a.** The Blue and the Red
   - **b.** The White and the Yellow
   - **c.** The Yellow and the Black
   - **d.** The White and the Blue

3. Baikal is the biggest __________ in the world.
   - **a.** saltwater lake
   - **b.** freshwater river
   - **c.** freshwater lake
   - **d.** freshwater sea

4. Victoria Falls is the name of the biggest __________ on earth.
   - **a.** mountain
   - **b.** island
   - **c.** beach
   - **d.** waterfall

UNIT 9

On Campus

1. Do you like your university? Why or why not?
2. What's the most difficult subject for you?
3. Are grades important to you?

Expressions

Listen and write the correct letters in the blanks. Track 59

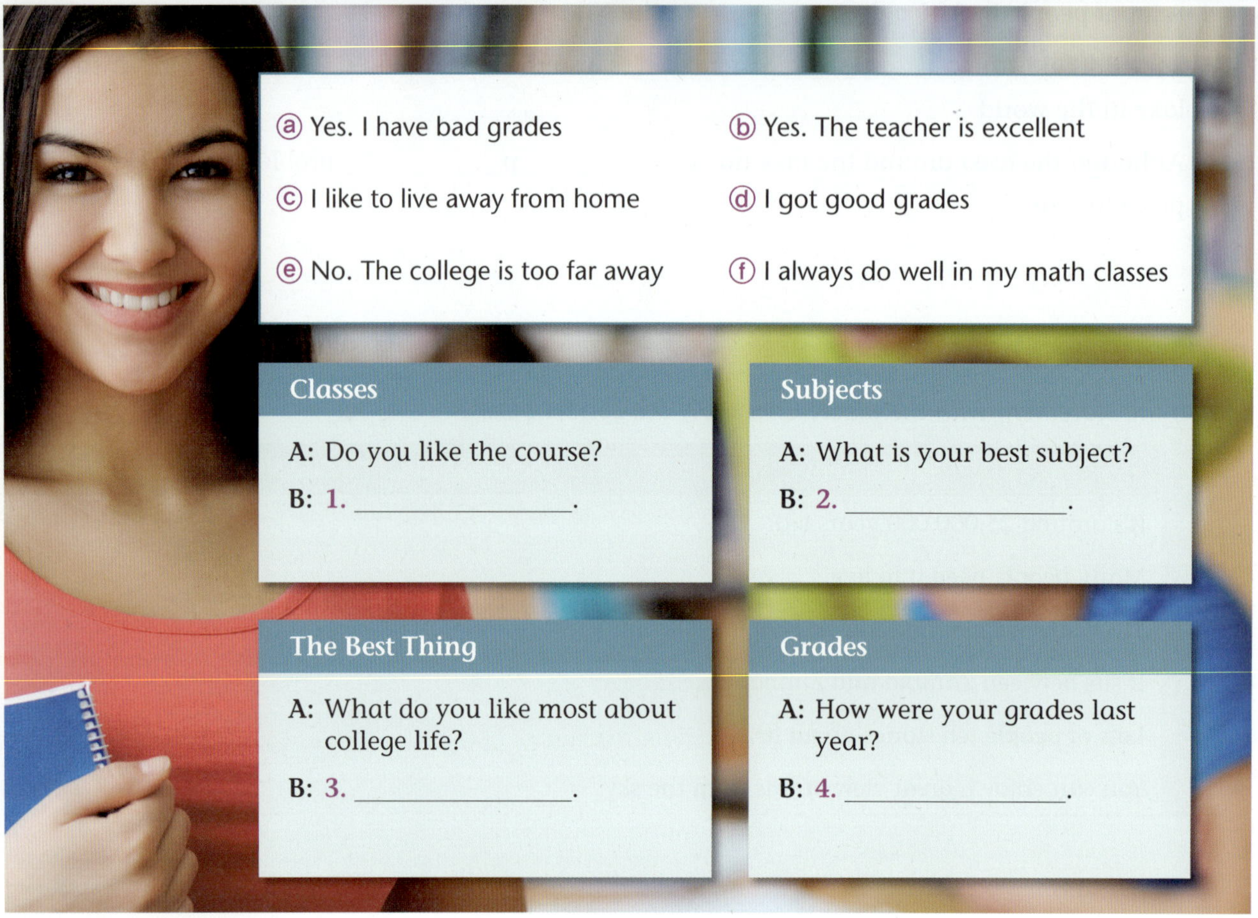

ⓐ Yes. I have bad grades

ⓑ Yes. The teacher is excellent

ⓒ I like to live away from home

ⓓ I got good grades

ⓔ No. The college is too far away

ⓕ I always do well in my math classes

Classes

A: Do you like the course?

B: 1. ______________.

Subjects

A: What is your best subject?

B: 2. ______________.

The Best Thing

A: What do you like most about college life?

B: 3. ______________.

Grades

A: How were your grades last year?

B: 4. ______________.

Small Talk

Practice the dialogues above using these expressions.

Classes

No. It's too basic.
No. It's too hard.
Yes. I really enjoy it.
Yes. My classmates are great.

Subjects

My strongest subject is English.
I am good at history.
I'm good at many different subjects.

The Best Thing

We don't need to wear uniforms.
I can meet people from different places.
I get to choose my classes.

Grades

I had terrible grades.
I got low grades.
My scores were high.

Words

Listen and repeat the words. Track 60

1 
course *n.*

2 
report *n.*

3 
semester *n.*

4 
final exam *n.*

5 
review *v.*

6 
prepare *v.*

7 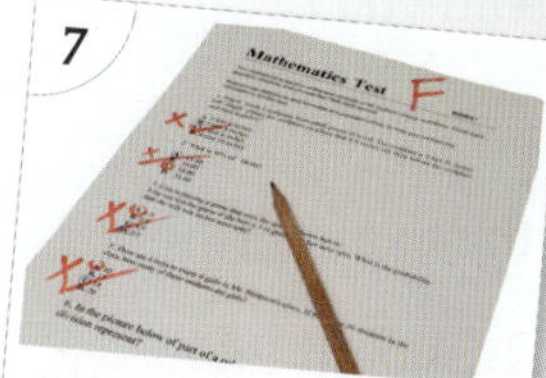
fail *v.*

8 
pass *v.*

Act It Out

Practice talking about ***college*** *with a partner.*

Question	Response
Is your math course difficult?	No. It's easy to pass. Yes. Lots of people fail. Yes. You have to study hard to get a good grade.
Do you have a lot of schoolwork right now?	Yes. I need to study for my final exams. Yes. I have to prepare a report this week. No. I just need to review the notes. Yes. I have a lot of courses this semester.

Listen Up

Task I *Listen and complete the sentences with the words you hear.* Track 61

1. Johnny likes his history ___________. It's really ___________.
2. The teacher knows a lot about the ___________.
3. Martha is worried about the ___________ ___________. She doesn't want to ___________ the class.
4. She also needs to ___________ a business report.

Task II *Match the word in bold with its synonym.*

course •	• test
grade •	• score
fail •	• study again
exam •	• class
review •	• not pass a test

Conversation

Test Trouble

Mark and Simon are at the library. Track 62

Mark: Hey, Simon! How are you?

Simon: I'm not so good, Mark. I just got my exam **results**.[1]

Mark: What **happened**?[2] Did you get a bad grade?

Simon: Yes. I failed.

Mark: I didn't do well on the exam **either**.[3] I passed, though.

Simon: This is terrible! What should I do?

Mark: It's not a big deal. It's just one exam. Did you study for it?

Simon: I did! The exam was just too difficult.

Mark: You can try to **improve**[4] your study **skills**.[5] How did you study?

Simon: I just started reading the book the day before the exam.

Mark: That's not very **responsible**.[6] You should change your study **habits**.[7] You need to review a little every day.

Simon: Why didn't you get a good grade?

Mark: I didn't study enough either. I'm too **lazy**.[8]

Simon: Let's review together next time.

Mark: Good idea. We can help each other.

Role Play

Use the words to make your own conversations.

History Exam	Driving Test	Writing Exam
failed	passed	passed
terrible	great	wonderful
hard	easy	not too difficult
55%	95%	92%

A: Did you pass your ___________?

B: ___________. I ___________ it.

A: Really? That's ___________ (adj.).

B: I know. It was ___________ (adj.).

A: What was your grade?

B: I got ___________ percent.

A. Key Words Track 63

1. **result** *n.* Jim's test results are always good. He's a great student.	2. **happen** *v.* Something is happening outside. I can hear some noise.
3. **either** *adv.* Becky doesn't speak French. I don't speak French either.	4. **improve** *v.* You need to improve your driving. It's scary.
5. **skill** *n.* He plays basketball very well. He has excellent skills.	6. **responsible** *adj.* Mike is responsible. I can always trust him.
7. **habit** *n.* Smoking is a bad habit. You should quit.	8. **lazy** *adj.* I'm lazy on weekends. I just like to stay home.

B. Listening Key Track 64

Listen and complete the sentences with the words you hear.

1. Frank is busy. Jared doesn't have much time ___________.
2. Frank is ___________ ___________ a student meeting.
3. The students want to ___________ college life.
4. Jared tells Frank not to ___________ ___________ the exam.
5. Frank needs a good ___________ on the exam.

C. Language Tips

1. The Usage of *Either*

Subject + Verb + not + either	agree with a negative statement	**A:** I failed the exam. **B:** I didn't do well either.
either A or B	give choices	**A:** We can take either a bus or a taxi. **B:** Let's take a taxi. It's faster.

Put the words in the correct order.

1. We / or / see / can / a movie. / either / to / a club / go ▶ ___________
2. I / doesn't / Leo / don't either. / a / have /pet. ▶ ___________
3. isn't / Pam / to / I / eat / want / don't / either. / anything / hungry. ▶ ___________
4. either / You / noodles / choose / or / can / rice. ▶ ___________

2. Cheering People Up

It's not a big deal.	It's not the end of the world.	Don't worry about it.

Fill in the blanks and practice speaking these sentences with a partner.

1. **A:** I don't like my job!
   B: ___________. You can get another one.
2. **A:** I can't find my notes.
   B: ___________. You can borrow mine.

Grammar

The Simple Past

Be Verbs

Statements

Affirmative			Negative		
Subject	Be Verb		Subject	Be Verb + Not	
I / He / She / It	was	in the house.	I / He / She / It	wasn't	in the house.
We / You / They	were	very happy.	We / You / They	weren't	very happy.

Questions

Question	Response
Was the exam difficult?	Yes. Some of the questions were really hard.
When were Tommy and his friends here?	They were here at 6 a.m.

Verbs

Statements

Affirmative		Negative		
Subject	Past Form of Verb	Subject	Did Not	Base Form of Verb
I / You / He / She / It / We / They	passed. went away.	I / You / He / She / It / We / They	didn't	pass. go away.

Questions

Question	Response
Did you get a bad grade?	Yes. I failed.
How did you study?	I just started reading the book the day before the exam.

The Past Form

	Verb Ending	Spelling	Example
Regular	–e	add **–d**	organize → organized
	consonant + –y	change **–y** to **–ied**	study → studied
	one vowel + one consonant	repeat the consonant, add **–ed**	stop → stopped
	others	add **–ed**	happen → happened
Irregular	get → got do → did	eat → ate have → had	read → read

A. Make Sentences

*Change the sentences into the **simple past tense**.*

1. Gary runs 10 kilometers every day. (yesterday)
   ▶ ____________________________________.
2. The boys practice baseball a lot. (last summer)
   ▶ ____________________________________.
3. She is very sad today. (this morning)
   ▶ ____________________________________.
4. Are the books on the shelf? (a week ago)
   ▶ ____________________________________?
5. Do you go to that restaurant? (last week)
   ▶ ____________________________________?

B. Match

Match the question with the response.

_____ **1.** Did he play the guitar?

_____ **2.** Where were the keys?

_____ **3.** When did you meet with Stephanie?

_____ **4.** Did you bring any money?

_____ **5.** What did Calvin tell you?

_____ **6.** Why were you in the forest?

_____ **7.** Did you go on vacation last year?

a. He didn't say anything.

b. I saw her last night.

c. I wanted to go for a walk.

d. No, he didn't. He was a singer.

e. Yes. I went to New York.

f. They were in my pocket.

g. Yes. I had $20.

C. Complete the Passage

Use the correct form of the verbs in parentheses to complete the passage. Use contractions if possible.

Dear Steve,

France **1.** _________(be) wonderful! Last week, the weather **2.** _________(be) great. It **3.** _________ _________(not rain) once. We **4.** _________(walk) in the countryside and **5.** _________(drink) wine. Yesterday, we **6.** _________(get) to Paris. We **7.** _________(go) to the Louvre. Some of the paintings **8.** _________(be) beautiful. Last night, we **9.** _________ (have) coffee near Notre Dame and **10.** _________(listen) to some jazz music. We really **11.** _________(enjoy) our evening. We **12.** _________(eat) breakfast in the hotel this morning. I **13.** _________ (love) French food!

Love,

Karl R.

To: Steve Dunleavy
1211, Sixth Ave.,
New York, USA

Reading

Before You Read

Look at the pictures. What are these people doing? What do you think the reading is about?

Bedroom Classroom

Track 65

While You Read

1. How many people study online in the U.S.?
2. Why are online courses cheaper for students?
3. What is the best way to study?

In the past, going to college was about leaving home, living on campus, studying at the library, and going to parties. Now, more and more students are studying online. More than five million students in the U.S. are taking online classes. This number keeps growing every year. These days, 30 percent of new students choose to study online. Why is it so popular? First of all, students can study at home. This is cheaper for most students because they don't need to pay for rent or travel. Secondly, it's easy to start taking online classes. Around 66 percent of U.S. universities offer online courses. Also, for some students it's an easier way to learn. Students get better grades when they study online than in the classroom. However, the best results come from doing some online work and some classroom work at the same time. How about you? Do you make your bedroom your classroom?

Extra Info

Students in Online Courses

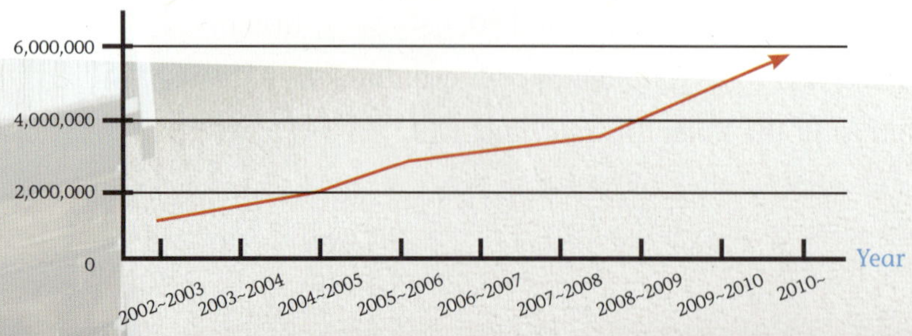

A. Fill in the Missing Letters

Complete the sentences with the words from the article.

1. In the past, students left home to go to **c**__________.
2. Students lived on **c**__________ in the past.
3. Now, more people are taking **o**__________ classes.
4. Studying at home is very **p**__________ today.
5. Many new students **c**__________ to study online these days.
6. Online classes are **c**__________ because students can save money on **r**__________ or **t**__________.
7. Lots of schools **o**__________ this type of learning.
8. Doing some work online and some in class gets students the best **r**__________.

B. Find the Facts

Read and check (✓).

	According to the writer, online classes become popular because...	
1	Students need to leave their homes.	
2	Students can study in their rooms.	
3	It can be less expensive.	
4	Students have to pay for rent.	
5	It is easy to take online classes.	
6	It is the best way to learn to all students.	
7	The number of the students taking online classes is decreasing.	
8	Students get better grades.	

C. True or False

Check (✓) ***True*** *or* ***False****.*

	Statement	True	False
1	More people study online every year.		
2	More than a half of the students study online.		
3	Some students still study in classrooms.		
4	Students can mix classroom work and online study.		
5	There are five million people in the U.S.		
6	Every university in the U.S. has online courses.		
7	Learning from home saves time and money.		

UNIT 10

Happy Times

1. What is the happiest time of the year for you?
2. What do you do on your birthday?
3. How do you prepare for the Lunar New Year?

Expressions

Listen and write the correct letters in the blanks. Track 66

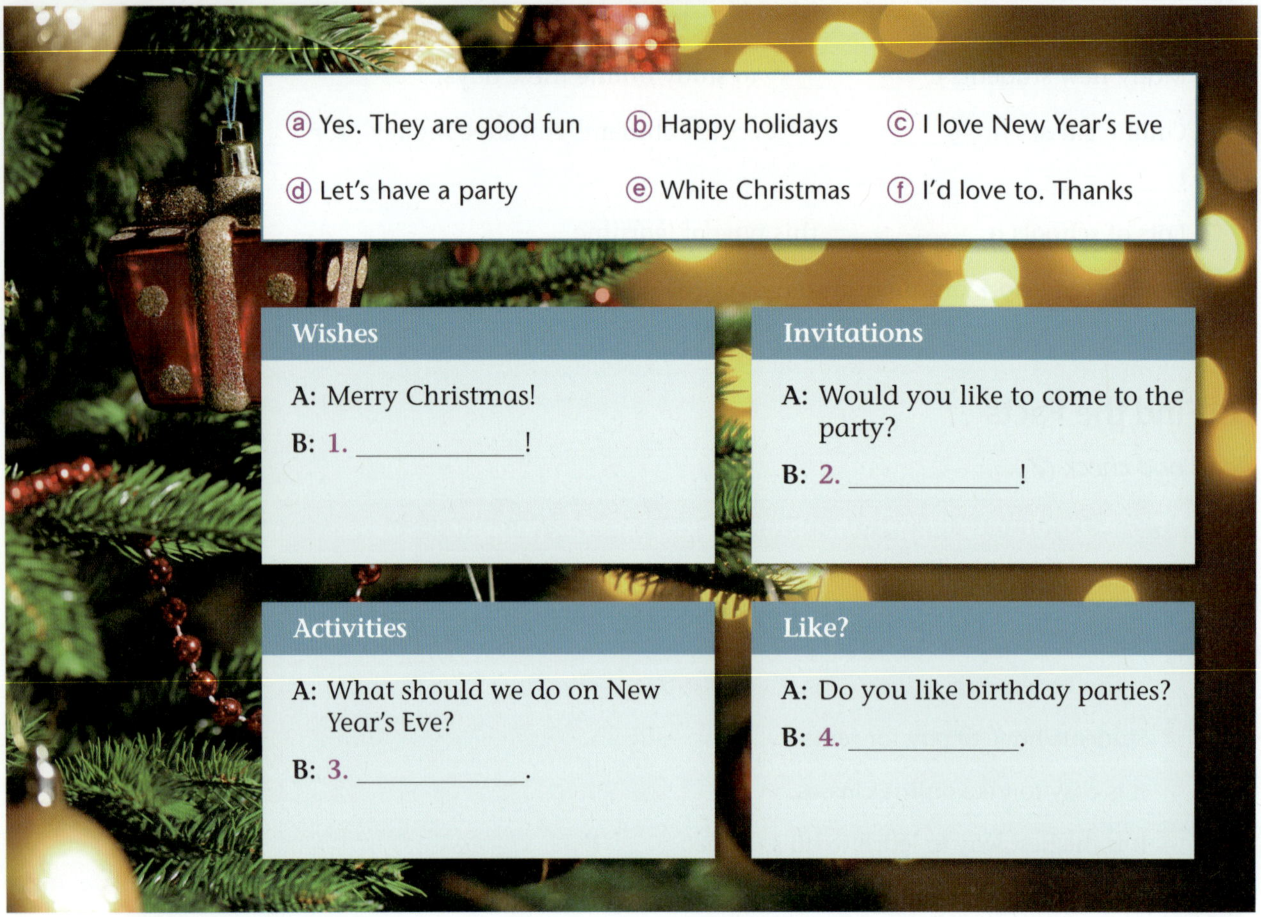

ⓐ Yes. They are good fun ⓑ Happy holidays ⓒ I love New Year's Eve

ⓓ Let's have a party ⓔ White Christmas ⓕ I'd love to. Thanks

Wishes

A: Merry Christmas!

B: 1. ____________!

Invitations

A: Would you like to come to the party?

B: 2. ____________!

Activities

A: What should we do on New Year's Eve?

B: 3. ____________.

Like?

A: Do you like birthday parties?

B: 4. ____________.

Small Talk *Practice the dialogues above using these expressions.*

Wishes

(Birthday) Happy birthday!
(January 1st) Happy New Year!
(Wedding) Best wishes!

Invitations

That sounds great.
Sure. What time?
I'm sorry. I can't.

Activities

We could go to a club.
Let's eat at a nice restaurant.
We should go see a movie.

Like?

Yes. I love to see all my friends together.
Yes. I like food and drink.
No. I'm too shy for parties.

Words

Listen and repeat the words. Track 67

1

welcome *v.*

2

invite *v.*

3

dress up *phr.*

4

decorate *v.*

5

holiday *n.*

6

surprise *n.*

7

present *n.*

8

guest *n.*

Act It Out

*Practice talking about **special days** with a partner.*

Question	Response
What do you do on Christmas?	I spend the holiday with my family. I buy a Christmas tree and decorate my house.
What do you need to do for the party?	I have to invite my friends. I need to welcome the guests. I have to dress up.
Do you like to get presents?	Yes. I love surprises. No. I prefer to get money.

Listen Up

*Listen and check (✓) **True** or **False**.* Track 68

	Statement	True	False
1	Paul's birthday is next month.		
2	Colin usually likes parties. He thinks they're fun.		
3	Ryan wants to organize a party.		
4	They tell Paul everything about the party.		
5	Ryan likes to wear his nicest clothes.		

Conversation

The Big Party

Glenn and Judy are talking on campus. Track 69

Glenn: Judy, are you free on Wednesday, June sixth?

Judy: Why, Glenn? Is there a party?

Glenn: It's my brother's **wedding**[1] day. Would you like to come with me?

Judy: At what time? I have to go to class that day.

Glenn: It's at 12 o'clock, but we need to **arrive**[2] before 11:30 a.m.

Judy: That should be fine. I have a class at 9:00 a.m., but it finishes at 10:30 a.m.

Glenn: Great! **I booked**[3] a jazz **band.**[4] They are excellent.

Judy: Sounds fun! Should I dress up?

Glenn: Yes. It's a **formal**[5] party. Girls should wear **dresses,**[6] and guys should wear **suits.**[7]

Judy: Did you invite many guests?

Glenn: Yeah. We invited all of our **relatives.**[8]

Judy: How about your cousin?

Glenn: My cousin isn't able to **attend.**[9] He's in South Africa.

Judy: That's too bad. He's really cute!

Role Play

Use the words to make your own conversations.

Event	my uncle's wedding	a New Year's Eve party
Date	March 11th	December 31st
Time	noon	6 p.m.
Clothes	wear formal clothes	dress up a little

A: Would you like to attend ____________ (event) with me?

B: When is it?

A: It's on ____________(date) at ____________(time).

B: I'd love to. What should I wear?

A: You should ____________(clothes).

B: Sounds good!

A. Key Words Track 70

1. **wedding** *n.* She went to Henry and Clara's wedding.	2. **arrive** *v.* They arrived at their hotel early in the morning.
3. **book** *v.* I booked a famous piano player for my dinner party.	4. **band** *n.* My favorite band comes from South Korea. I listen to their songs every day.
5. **formal** *adj.* This is a formal dinner. You can't wear jeans.	6. **dress** *n.* Your yellow dress is beautiful. It looks great on you.
7. **suit** *n.* Joe usually wears a suit and tie to work.	8. **relative** *n.* Lisa has relatives in Boston. Her grandmother and uncle live there.
9. **attend** *v.* I attended a great show last Wednesday.	

B. Listening Key Track 71

Listen and complete the sentences with the words you hear.

1. Sue's ____________ party is ____________ the fourth of ____________.
2. Sophia ____________ ____________ Danny to go with her to the party.
3. Danny has to go to a ____________ of one of his ____________.
4. It is a ____________ event.
5. He bought a ____________ for the party.

C. Language Tips

1. Invitations

↓	Do you want to . . .?	Do you want to come with me?
	Are you interested in + Verb + -ing . . .?	Are you interested in coming with me?
most polite	Would you like to . . .?	Would you like to come with me?

Practice saying the questions above with the words below. Change the verb form if necessary.

go bowling	learn the guitar	go to the gym	have lunch

2. The Usage of *Be Able to*

Meaning	Example
Be able to can be used to talk about ability, but **can** is more common.	I am able to make a cake. = I can make a cake.
	Kate is able to speak French like a native. = Kate can speak French like a native.

Grammar

Expressing Time

Prepositions

Preposition	Usage	Example
at	clock time	The wedding is at 12 o'clock. I have a class at 9 a.m.
on	days of the week dates	Mother's Day is on Sunday. His birthday is on June sixth.
in	months years seasons	Many flowers grow in May. I visited New York in 2005. It is warmer in spring.
after	any time word	She arrived after 11 p.m.
before	any time word	Please finish this before lunch.
between	two points in time	Dinner hours are between 6:00 and 9:30.

Usage Note

When we talk about **dates**, we usually say the month first and then an ordinal number.

Cardinal	one	two	three	four	five
Ordinal	first (1st)	second (2nd)	third (3rd)	fourth (4th)	fifth (5th)

Cardinal	six	seven	eight	nine	ten
Ordinal	sixth (6th)	seventh (7th)	eighth (8th)	ninth (9th)	tenth (10th)

Expressions

Expression	Example
at noon / night	He likes to read books at night.
in the morning / afternoon / evening	Amy drinks coffee in the morning.
on (day) morning / afternoon / evening / night	We watched a movie on Friday night.
on weekends	Jim goes fishing on weekends.

Usage Note

We don't use **at**, **on**, or **in** in the following situations.

Jerry went home **last** month.

We can go running **next** week.

I eat breakfast **every** morning.

A. Fill in the Blanks

Use the words ***at, on, in, after, before, between, every*** *to complete the sentences.*

1. Harold always arrives early __________ the morning.
2. We meet __________ Mondays and play cards.
3. I must be home __________ dinner. I need to help my mother cook.
4. Amanda works __________ the afternoon, __________ 2:00 and 6:00.
5. My dad often watches sports __________ the evening __________ work.
6. Judy visits her grandparents __________ Wednesday.
7. We take a lunch break __________ noon.
8. I usually sleep late __________ weekends.

B. Match

Match the question with the response.

_____ 1. When did Susan leave?	a. It's on July 11th.
_____ 2. What time does he finish work?	b. He was there in 2013.
_____ 3. Do you want to see a movie sometime?	c. He leaves the office at 6 p.m.
_____ 4. When does your father go to sleep?	d. No. I have to meet my friend after dinner tonight.
_____ 5. Are you free tonight?	e. She left before noon.
_____ 6. Does your sister have to go to school today?	f. He goes to bed after the evening news.
_____ 7. When is Joe's birthday?	g. Yes. She has a class between 12:00 and 3:00.
_____ 8. When did Sam study in Paris?	h. Sure. Let's go on Saturday afternoon.

C. Complete the Passage

Use the word choices given to complete the passage.

between	on	in	at	after

Alexander Graham Bell is known for his invention of the telephone. However, he was not the first inventor of the telephone.

Antonio Meucci made the world's first phone **1.** ________ 1849. Meucci was born **2.** ________ April 13th, 1808. When he was young, he worked in Cuba. **3.** ________ many years, he moved to America. **4.** ________ 1856 and 1870, Meucci made 30 phones. However, his invention was not successful.

5. ________ 1876, Bell invented the first telephone and applied for a patent. Meucci died **6.** ________ noon **7.** ________ October 18th, 1889. He was poor, and nobody knew his name.

Reading

Before You Read

Look at the pictures. Where can you go to see these scenes? What do you think the reading is about?

The World's Biggest Party

Track 72

While You Read

1. What is special about the World Cup?

2. Who celebrates the World Cup?

3. How many teams play in the World Cup?

People all over the world celebrate the FIFA(Fédération Internationale dé Football Association) World Cup finals for a whole month. It is the biggest sports event in the world. Soccer teams from different countries play each other. There are 32 teams in the World Cup finals. The event happens every four years in the summer. Many countries want to host the games because the World Cup finals bring in visitors and money. There are parties on the streets everywhere. Fans all want to see the games and cheer. Of course, not everyone can go to the matches. Many people enjoy World Cup parties at their homes or in bars. People watch the match and sing, dance, cry, and drink together. Try to find a World Cup party during the next World Cup finals. They're always a lot of fun!

Extra Info

About the World Cup

About the World Cup
The first World Cup was in 1930 in Uruguay.
In 2002, South Korea and Japan hosted the World Cup together.
Brazil won the World Cup five times.
Mario Mendez was the youngest player in the World Cup history. He was 16.

A. Fill in the Missing Letters

Complete the sentences with the words from the article.

1. The FIFA World Cup is the biggest sports e__________ in the world.
2. People in every country c__________ the sport for a w__________ month.
3. 32 soccer t__________ from around the world join the World Cup f__________.
4. Many countries want to h__________ the World Cup to bring in v__________ and earn m__________.
5. Many soccer fans go to the games and c__________.
6. People have World Cup parties at home, in b__________, and on the s__________.

B. Fill in the Blanks

Use the correct form of the word choices given to complete the sentences.

year	fan	team	host	summer	1930	happen	fun

World Cup Fast Facts

1. 32 __________ play each other in the finals.
2. The World Cup __________ every four __________ in the __________.
3. World Cup __________ sing, cheer, and drink together.
4. People have a lot of __________ at World Cup parties.
5. Uruguay __________ the first World Cup in __________.

C. Multiple Choice

Circle the answers.

1. How long are the World Cup finals?
   a. Six weeks
   b. Four days
   c. One month
   d. Two years

2. Why do countries want to host the World Cup?
   a. Many people visit the country.
   b. The country gets better players.
   c. The country might win the finals.
   d. People want to be on TV.

3. What do people do at a World Cup party?
   a. People host the World Cup.
   b. People cheer and watch the game.
   c. People get married and travel.
   d. People play soccer.

4. Where might you find a World Cup party?
   a. At a bar
   b. At someone's house
   c. On a city street
   d. All of the above

5. What countries hosted the World Cup at the same time?
   a. South Korea and China
   b. Japan and Taiwan
   c. France and England
   d. Japan and South Korea

UNIT 11

Food to Go

1. What's your favorite food?
2. Where do you like to eat?
3. Do you like fast food?

Expressions

Listen and write the correct letters in the blanks. **Track 73**

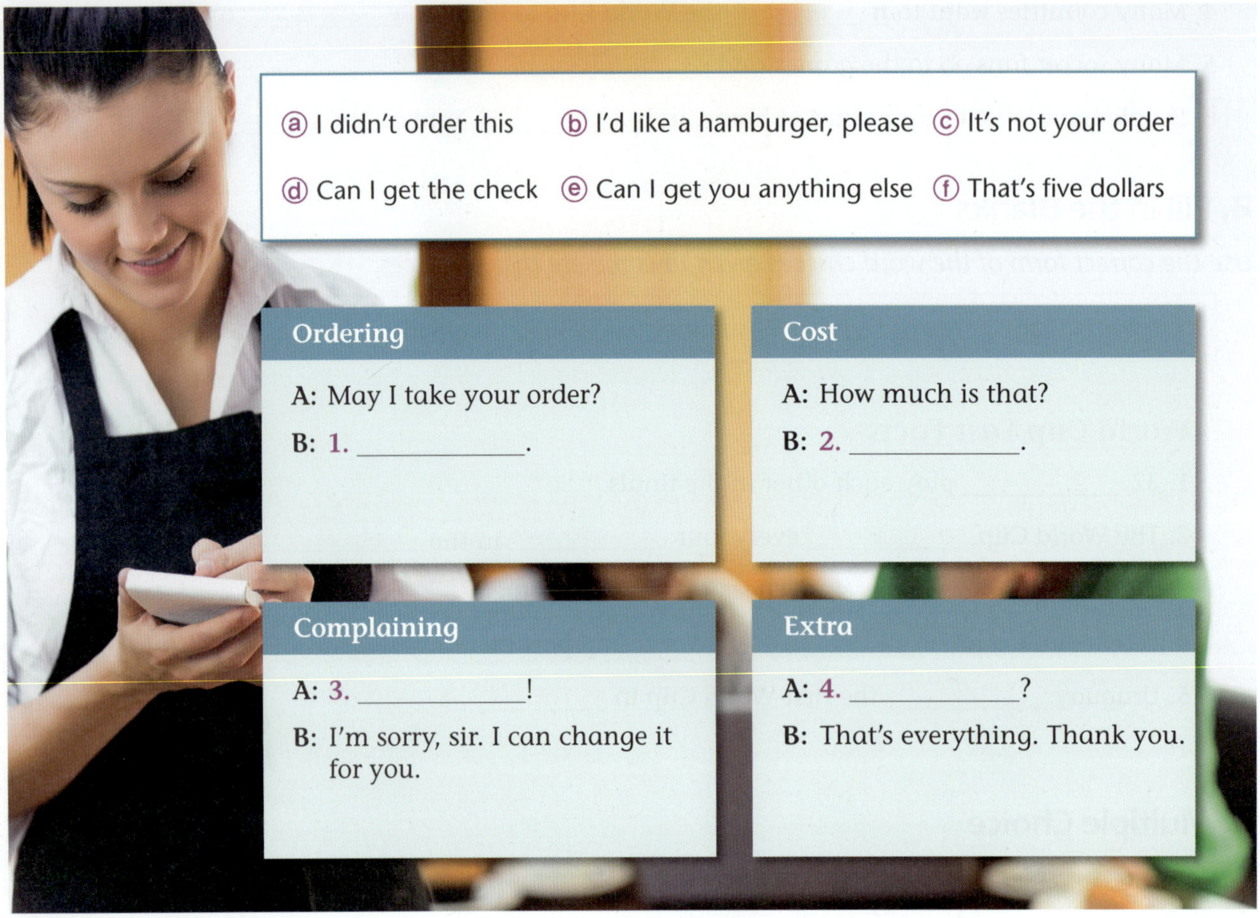

ⓐ I didn't order this ⓑ I'd like a hamburger, please ⓒ It's not your order

ⓓ Can I get the check ⓔ Can I get you anything else ⓕ That's five dollars

Ordering

A: May I take your order?

B: 1. ____________.

Cost

A: How much is that?

B: 2. ____________.

Complaining

A: 3. ____________!

B: I'm sorry, sir. I can change it for you.

Extra

A: 4. ____________?

B: That's everything. Thank you.

Small Talk

Practice the dialogues above using these expressions.

Ordering

I want two doughnuts.
I'd like a salad.
Could I have another minute, please?

Cost

The total is eight dollars.
That's a total of nine dollars.

Complaining

This isn't my order.
My burger is cold.
This fork is dirty.

Extra

Would you like anything else?
Is that everything?
Is there anything else?

Words

Listen and repeat the words. Track 74

1 **deliver** *v.*

2 **order** *v.*

3 **extra** *adj.*

4 **medium** *adj.*

5 **beef** *n.*

6 **change** *n.*

7 **fries** *n.*

8 **ketchup** *n.*

Act It Out

Practice talking about ***ordering*** *with a partner.*

Question	Response
Do you deliver?	Sure. What do you want to order? I'm sorry. We don't deliver.
Is that my order?	Yes, it is. And here's your bill. Yes. These fries are yours. Yes. This is your medium Coke. Yes, sir. Here is your beef burger with extra ketchup.

Listen Up

Task I *Listen and check (✓) the correct boxes.* Track 75

STEP 1	STEP 2	STEP 3
Choose a Pizza	**Choose toppings**	**Anything else?**
☐ small	☐ chicken	☐ extra cheese
☐ medium	☐ ham	☐ extra tomatoes
☐ large	☐ beef	

Task II *Listen again and complete the sentences with the words you hear.*

1. Simon can't decide between __________ and __________.
2. They __________ over the phone.
3. Tommy's Pizza can __________ to their house on Pine Road.
4. They want more __________ on their pizza.

Conversation

Breakfast Sandwich

Sam meets Marcy in the morning. Track 76

Marcy: Hey, Sam. Do you want to go for breakfast?

Sam: OK, Marcy. Where would you like to go?

Marcy: Let's go to the sandwich shop. It's just around the **corner**.[1]

Sam: Great. I'm really hungry.

(at the shop)

Waitress:[2] Good morning. May I take your order?

Sam: I'd like an egg sandwich with ketchup, please.

Waitress: Anything to drink?

Sam: I'd like a **soda**.[3]

Waitress: Small, medium, or large?

Sam: Medium.

Marcy: Just a small strawberry **shake**[4] for me.

Sam: You look **thin**.[5] You should have something to eat!

Marcy: You're right. I want an egg sandwich too, please.

Waitress: No problem. Two sandwiches, a soda, and a shake. The **total**[6] is $14.

Marcy: Here you go.

Waitress: Thanks. Here's your change. Give me five minutes. Have a **seat**.[7]

Sam: She's very **friendly**.[8]

Marcy: Yes. I come in here a lot.

Waitress: Here's your order.

Marcy: Thanks!

Sam: Bye!

Role Play *Use the words to make your own conversations.*

	Big Burger	Maria's Café
What	a fish burger and fries	a salad and a milk
Size	fries — *small*	milk — *medium*
Cost	$4.00	$5.10

A: Hello! Welcome to ____________.
Can I take your order?

B: Hi! I'd like ____________, please.

A: OK. What size ____________ would you like?

B: ____________(size), please.

A: The total is ____________.

B: Here you go. Thanks!

A. Key Words Track 77

1. **corner** *n.* My house is on the corner of Abbey Street and Fifth Street.	2. **waitress** *n.* Julie is a waitress at the pizza restaurant.
3. **soda** *n.* I usually have a soda with my lunch.	4. **shake** *n.* (milk shake) Ted loves to drink chocolate shakes.
5. **thin** *adj.* It's not healthy to be too thin.	6. **total** *n.* We have a total of 28 students in our history class.
7. **seat** *n.* There are 50 seats on the bus.	8. **friendly** *adj.* May's parents are very friendly. They always invite me to dinner.

B. Listening Key Track 78

Listen and complete the sentences with the words you hear.

1. Gary asks Tony to ____________ him a ____________.
2. Gary is not being very ____________ to Tony.
3. Gary tells Tony to have a ____________.
4. Gary is ____________ a chocolate milk ____________.
5. Tony would like to drink a ____________.
6. The bread is in the ____________.

C. Language Tips

1. The Usage of *Just*

Meaning	Example
close to (short distance)	It's just around the corner.
only	I just want a small strawberry shake.

Check (✓) the correct usage.

1. We **just** need five dollars. ☐ Close to ☐ Only
2. Could you give me my bag? It's **just** beside you. ☐ Close to ☐ Only

2. Asking Someone to Wait

Give me (*time*).	Wait (*time*).	Wait for (*time*).	Have / Take a seat.

Fill in the blanks.

1. I'm pretty busy right now. ______________(a few minutes).
2. ______________(a second). I'm on the telephone.
3. Sorry. Dr. Robinson is not ready. Please ______________ in the waiting room.

Grammar

Adjectives

Adjectives give more information about nouns. They always keep the same form.

Positions

Before nouns	The green coat is on the table.
After be verbs	I'm hungry. You're right. The waitress is friendly.
After sensing verbs	You look thin.

Types

Type	Adjective	Example
article	a, an, the	I want a soda.
possessive	my, his, their, your . . .	May I take your order?
demonstrative	this, that, these, those	Those books are Frank's.
number	one, two, three . . .	Give me five minutes.
noun	sandwich, egg . . .	Let's go to the sandwich shop. I'd like an egg sandwich, please.
quality	blue, beautiful, young . . .	Where is the blue chair?

Usage Note

1. You can use more than one adjective to describe a noun.

   For Example:
   - her pretty new skirt
   - the big old yellow house

2. Some adjectives look like adverbs or verbs.

Ending	Adjective	Example
–ly	friendly lovely	She is a lovely girl.
–ed	excited bored	I'm really excited about the show tonight.
–ing	exciting boring	That movie is boring.

3. We use words like **very** and **really** to show the degree of the adjective.

   Dennis is **really** tired. He worked all day. (quality adjective)
   ~~There is a **very** movie theater behind the park.~~ (noun adjective)

A. Put in Order

Put the words in the correct order.

1. like / coffee. / would / I / hot / a / large

 ▶ ______________________________

2. have / They / a / big / the / comfortable house / in / countryside.

 ▶ ______________________________

3. really / right / It's / in / now. / Japan / cold

 ▶ ______________________________

4. are / There / hungry / cage. / three / in / cats / the

 ▶ ______________________________

5. sister. / is / as / Lucy / smart / her / as

 ▶ ______________________________

6. hair. / beautiful / has / Samantha / black

 ▶ ______________________________

B. Find the Adjectives

Circle the adjectives in the passage.

Travel Diary

April 18th

I'm in Dublin this week. I'm visiting some of the most famous places in Ireland. Trinity College is the oldest university in Ireland. The campus is beautiful and green. There are huge old trees everywhere. It's so quiet, but the busy city streets are right outside! The school library is interesting too. They keep lots of old books there. *The Book of Kells* is over 1,200 years old. It has lovely pictures and wonderful designs. The students look happy. I'd love to study here.

C. Correct the Mistakes

Fix the errors in the sentences.

1. I like walking, but it's to cold to climb a mountain.

 ▶ ______________________________

2. Those dogs little are so loud. Big dogs are more quieter.

 ▶ ______________________________

3. Jenny gave me a quicks smile before she left.

 ▶ ______________________________

4. Eve is the girl with big eyes blue.

 ▶ ______________________________

5. That car looks nicely, but it very expensive.

 ▶ ______________________________

Reading

Before You Read

What do you see in each picture? What do you think the reading is about?

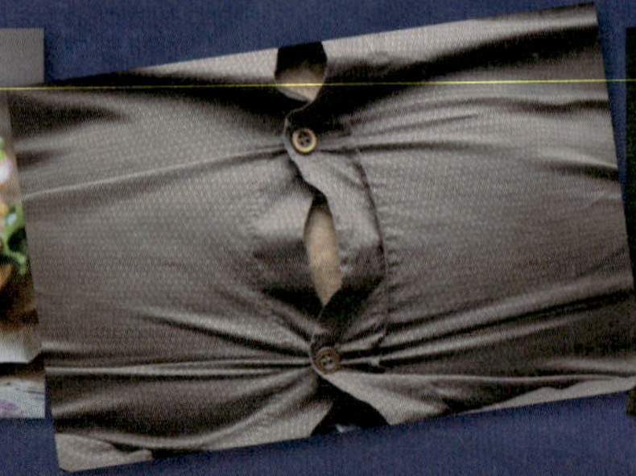

Your Size and French Fries

Track 79

While You Read

1. *What is the movie Super Size Me about?*
2. *How did Spurlock feel when he ate lots of fast food?*
3. *How much weight did Spurlock gain?*

What happens when you eat only fast food for one month? In 2003, Morgan Spurlock decided to make a movie about fast food in America. The movie is called *Super Size Me*. It shows the effects of fast food on the body. For a full month, Spurlock ate at McDonald's three times a day. He tried everything on the menu. He often had big meals. During this time, Spurlock was often tired and lacked energy. He felt bad all the time. He had heart problems too. His doctors were very worried. Spurlock gained more than 11 kilograms in the month when he ate only McDonald's. He became pretty fat. It took Spurlock more than a year to lose that weight. The movie warns people about the dangers of fast food. It's also a clever, funny movie. It was famous around the world.

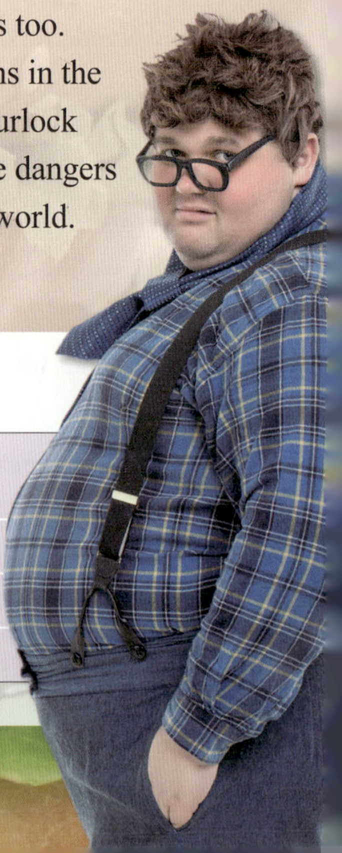

Extra Info

About Fast Food

Fast food companies spend more than $4,000,000,000 every year on advertisements.
Children see 12,000 fast food advertisements a year on TV.
Every day, more than 46 million people eat at McDonald's.
Many burgers have more than 900 calories.

A. Fill in the Missing Letters

Complete the sentences with the words from the article.

1. Morgan Spurlock made a **m**__________ about the **e**__________ of fast food on health.
2. Spurlock had three **m**__________ a day at McDonald's for one **m**__________.
3. He tried everything on the **m**__________.
4. Fast food made Spurlock feel **t**__________. He didn't have any **e**__________.
5. Spurlock's doctors were **w**__________ about his **h**__________ problems.
6. He became pretty **f**__________ during that month. He **g**__________ over 11 kilograms.
7. The movie teaches us about the **d**__________ of fast food.

B. Complete the Chart

*Circle **Yes** or **No**.*

	What's true about Morgan Spurlock?		
1	He ate a lot of fast food in order to make a movie.	Yes	No
2	He got very thin.	Yes	No
3	He had some problems with his heart.	Yes	No
4	His movie is called *Super Size Me*.	Yes	No
5	He worked at McDonald's for one month.	Yes	No
6	It took him more than a year to lose the weight.	Yes	No
7	He ate the same meal every day.	Yes	No
8	His movie was famous.	Yes	No

C. Multiple Choice

Circle the answers.

1. What is the movie about?
   a. The dangers of fast food
   b. The causes of heart disease
   c. Ways to lose weight
   d. The history of McDonald's

2. For how long did Spurlock eat only McDonald's food?
   a. Around 11 years
   b. About 30 days
   c. One week
   d. One year

3. Why were Spurlock's doctors worried?
   a. They didn't like Spurlock.
   b. Spurlock had health problems.
   c. Spurlock didn't eat enough.
   d. Spurlock didn't pay the doctors.

4. What does the article say about the movie?
   a. It makes people lose weight.
   b. It's nothing to worry about.
   c. It is smart and interesting.
   d. It was good for McDonald's.

UNIT 12

On the Road

1. Do you like to travel? Why or why not?
2. How often do you go on vacation?
3. What's the best thing about traveling?

Expressions

Listen and write the correct letters in the blanks. Track 80

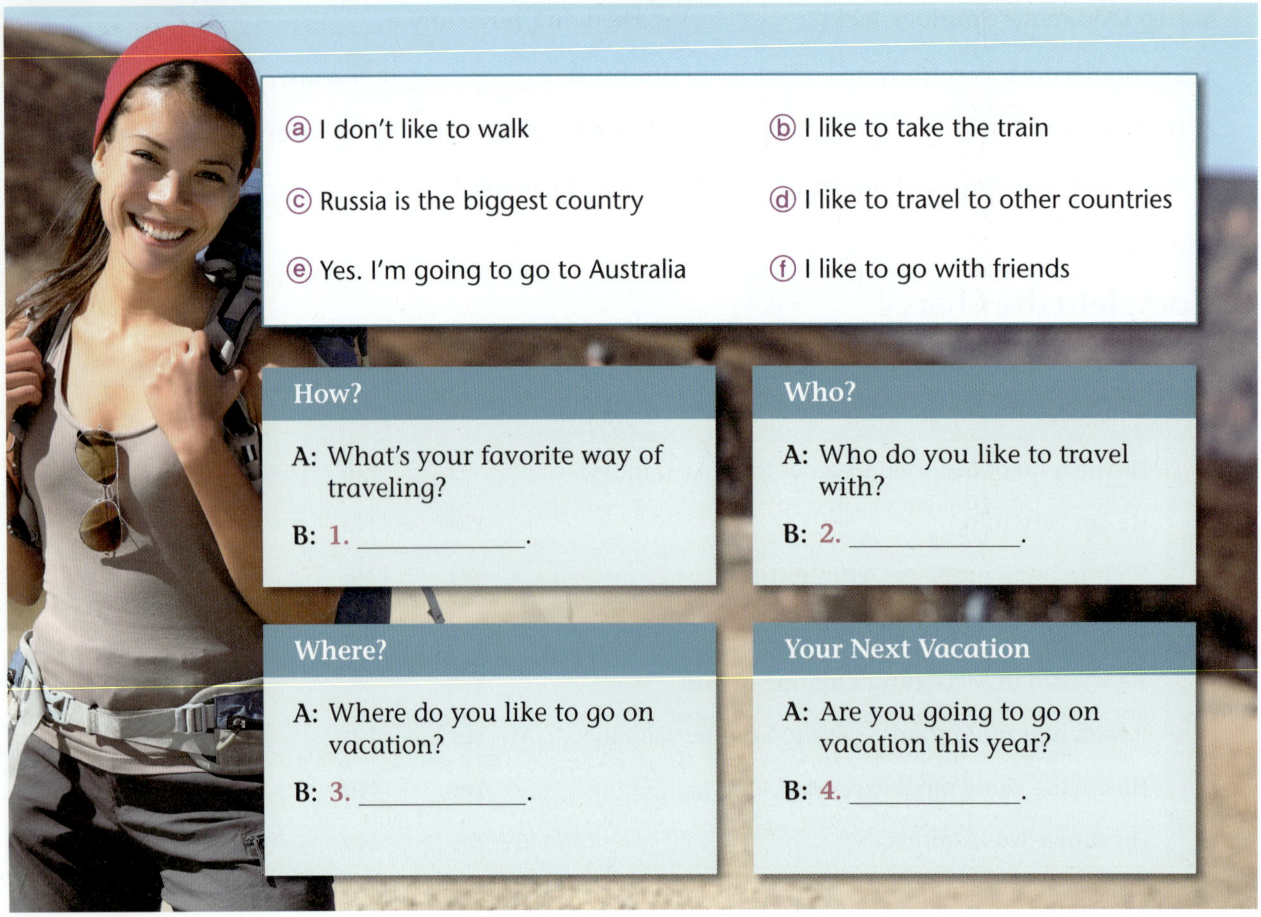

ⓐ I don't like to walk
ⓑ I like to take the train
ⓒ Russia is the biggest country
ⓓ I like to travel to other countries
ⓔ Yes. I'm going to go to Australia
ⓕ I like to go with friends

How?

A: What's your favorite way of traveling?

B: 1. ____________.

Who?

A: Who do you like to travel with?

B: 2. ____________.

Where?

A: Where do you like to go on vacation?

B: 3. ____________.

Your Next Vacation

A: Are you going to go on vacation this year?

B: 4. ____________.

Small Talk

Practice the dialogues above using these expressions.

How?

I like to go by airplane.
I enjoy driving.
Taking a bus is my favorite way to travel.

Who?

I prefer to travel alone.
I like traveling with my family.
I love to travel with my friends.

Where?

I like to go to the countryside.
I love city holidays.
I usually go to Europe.

Your Next Vacation

No. I don't have any plans.
Yes. I'm going to take a trip to Japan.
No. I'm not going to go away.

Words

Listen and repeat the words. Track 81

1 **visit** *v.*

2 **fly** *v.*

3 **ski** *v.*

4 **anywhere** *adv.*

5 **tour guide** *n.*

6 **tour group** *n.*

7 **postcard** *n.*

8 **abroad** *adv.*

Act It Out

Practice talking about ***traveling*** *with a partner.*

Question	Response
Which country do you want to visit most?	I really want to see France. I don't want to go anywhere abroad.
Do you like to travel with tour groups?	No. I like to plan my own trips. Yes. The tour guides know a lot.
What do you bring on vacation?	I always bring a map. I bring a book to read when I fly. I bring warm clothes.

Listen Up

Listen and check (✓) the correct choices. Track 82

Jessie's Trip		
When	☐ This winter	☐ Next summer
Who	☐ With a tour group	☐ By herself
How	☐ Take a plane	☐ Take a train
Where	☐ Australia	☐ Austria
Weather there	☐ Snowy	☐ Hot
What to do	☐ Go skiing	☐ See kangaroos

Conversation

Summer Work and Play

Will and Ted are talking about their plans for the summer. Track 83

Will: Hey, Ted! Are you busy this summer?

Ted: Hey, Will. I'm not **sure**[1] yet. I'm going to look for a job in New Zealand. How about you?

Will: I'm going to go to the Philippines for a **vacation**.[2]

Ted: The Philippines is **terrific**.[3]

Will: Yeah. A few of my friends are going too.

Ted: Sounds great. Do you have any plans?

Will: Yes. We're going to take a bus **tour**[4] and do a little swimming. I don't like group tours very much, though.

Ted: You're very **independent**,[5] right?

Will: Yes, but I **contacted**[6] my friend there. He's a guide. He's going to show us around. What are you going to do in New Zealand?

Ted: I'm going to **pick**[7] apples to make a few dollars. Then I'm going to **check out**[8] the mountains.

Will: Cool! **I hope**[9] you find a job!

Role Play

Use the words to make your own conversations.

Where	Thailand	Switzerland
When	in July	next week
What	go rock climbing	go skiing
	see elephants	eat chocolate

A: I'm going to go to ______________.

B: When are you going to go?

A: I'm going to go ______________.

B: Great! Are you going to ______________?

A: Yes. I'm going to ______________ too.

B: That sounds like a good vacation.

A. Key Words Track 84

1. **sure** *adj.* I'm not sure about the answer. You should ask Kenny.	2. **vacation** *n.* Audrey is not at work. She is on vacation in Paris.
3. **terrific** *adj.* This book is terrific! I'm really enjoying it.	4. **tour** *n.* We went on a tour of China for ten days.
5. **independent** *adj.* Tina is very independent. She does everything by herself.	6. **contact** *v.* You can contact me by e-mail or telephone.
7. **pick** *v.* We pick our tomatoes in early August.	8. **check out** *phr.* We should check out that movie.
9. **hope** *v.* I hope to study medicine in college.	

B. Listening Key Track 85

Listen and complete the sentences with the words you hear.

1. Nela is the guide on this ____________.
2. They are going to ____________ ____________ some of Italy's ____________ views.
3. They can be more ____________ in the afternoon.
4. The man wants to buy some ____________.
5. There are ____________ ____________ small shops in the area.

C. Language Tips

1. The Usage of *Yet*

The adverb **yet** means "at the present time." It is usually used in negative statements or questions.

I'm not sure **yet**. (= I don't know right now.)

Is my pizza ready **yet**? (= Is it ready now?)

2. A Few of vs. A Few

a few of + Noun	A few of my friends are going too.
a few + Noun	I'm going to pick apples to make a few dollars.

*Fill in the blanks with **a few of, a few,** or **very few.***

1. The new computer works well. There are ____________ problems.
2. I have ____________ calls to make. Give me 15 minutes.
3. ____________ my classmates are from other countries.

Usage Note

(Very) few is different from **a few**. It means "almost no."

A few people read his book. (A small number of people read his book.)

Very few people read his book. (Almost no one read his book.)

Grammar

Future: Be Going to

Statements

Subject + Be		(Not)	Going to	Base Form of Verb	(Time)
I	am	(not)	going to	look for a job.	
He / She / It	is	(not)	going to	help us	next week.
We / You / They	are	(not)	going to	play basketball	tomorrow.

Check for Pronunciation

*We often shorten the **be form** in speaking. Listen and circle the form you hear.* Track 86

1	They are / They're going to have a party.	2	He is / He's going to make dinner for us.
3	I am / I'm going to visit him this afternoon.	4	We are / We're going to leave at three o'clock.

Yes / No Questions

Question	Short Answer	Long Answer
Is Ted going to work when he is in New Zealand?	Yes, he is.	Yes. He's going to pick apples.
	No, he is not. No, he isn't.	No. He is not going to work when he is there.
Are Philip and Martin going to bring their friends?	Yes, they are.	Yes. They are going to bring some friends.
	No, they are not. No, they aren't.	No. Just the two of them are going to come.

Wh- Questions

Question	Response
What are they going to do there?	They're going to take a bus tour.
How is Will's friend going to help them?	He's going to show them around.
Where is Milly going to open her store?	She is going to open the store on Michael Street.

Other Tenses for the Future

Present Tense	When does your vacation start? (When is your vacation going to start?)
Present Continuous	Pamela is moving this weekend. (Pamela is going to move this weekend.)

A. Make Sentences

*Change the sentences into the future tense using **be going to**.*

1. She did well on her math exam. (next week)
   ▶ ____________________.
2. The guide showed me some nice places in New Zealand. (tomorrow)
   ▶ ____________________.
3. There were 500 people at the party. (on Saturday)
   ▶ ____________________.
4. Some of us went to the top of the mountain. (this afternoon)
   ▶ ____________________.
5. Arnold wrote a book about America. (next summer)
   ▶ ____________________.

B. Fill in the Blanks

Use the word choices given to complete the sentences.

is going to win	am going to leave	are going to feel
is . . . going to drive	are going to have	is . . . going to play

1. The trip sounds fun. The boys ____________ a great time.
2. Don't eat so much! You ____________ sick later.
3. ____________ your brother ____________ here? It's really far.
4. I ____________ in ten minutes. I have to go grocery shopping with my aunt.
5. Helena ____________ the tennis match. She's much better than Emily.
6. ____________ Todd ____________ the guitar? I'd love to hear that.

C. Match

Match the question / statement with the response.

_____ 1. Are you going to watch the movie with us?
_____ 2. When is your flight tomorrow?
_____ 3. It's going to rain in the afternoon.
_____ 4. Does Alan know about the test?
_____ 5. What are you going to wear to the party?
_____ 6. Does Terry have a coat?
_____ 7. Why is Hank wearing a swimsuit?
_____ 8. Are you going to finish work late today?

a. He's going to go to the beach.
b. I should bring an umbrella then.
c. Yes. I'm going to work late tonight.
d. No. He's going to be very cold.
e. It leaves at eight in the morning.
f. I don't know. I'm going to tell him.
g. No. I saw it last week.
h. I'm going to buy a new suit.

Before You Read

Look at the pictures. Where is the woman? What is special about her hotel? What do you think the reading is about?

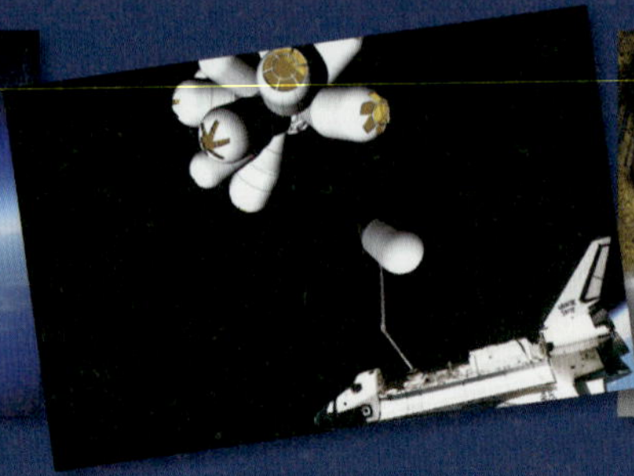

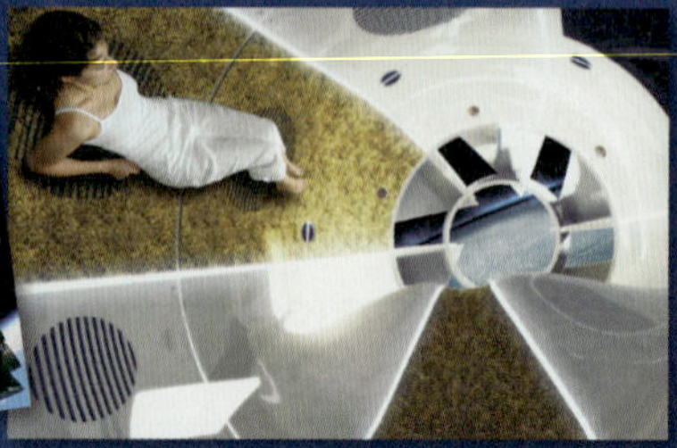

The First Hotel in Outer Space

Track 87

While You Read

1. What can visitors to outer space do?
2. How much does a trip to space cost?
3. How long can visitors stay in space?

Do you want a unique vacation? Go to outer space. You can stay in space for three days. First, you must train on an island for 16 weeks. Then, you take a spaceship to a space hotel. You can fly from room to room in the hotel. You can also look at the stars and watch the Earth from 450 kilometers up! From the hotel's view, the sun rises 15 times a day.

Very few people can go to outer space right now. Each spaceship only has six seats. These trips are also quite expensive. People must pay three million dollars for their vacation. Only around 40,000 people in the world can pay this. Space travel is probably going to become cheaper in the future, though. Even ordinary people may be able to travel to these hotels. You too could send your friends a postcard from space someday soon!

Extra Info

Space Firsts

First dog in space	1957	Laika
First man in space	1961	Yuri Gagarin
First woman in space	1963	Valentina Tereshkova
First man on the Moon	1969	Neil Armstrong
Longest space flight	2001	Valeri Polyakov (437 days)

Photos: Galactic Suite Design

A. Fill in the Missing Letters

Complete the sentences with the words from the article.

1. You can go to **o**__________ **s**__________ for a **u**__________ vacation.
2. First, you need to **t**__________ on an **i**__________ to go to outer space.
3. When you watch from the **h**__________, the sun **r**__________ 15 times a day.
4. Each **s**__________ only has six places to sit.
5. It is pretty **e**__________ to take the **t**__________.
6. In the future, **o**__________ people may be able to travel to these hotels and send **p**__________ to their friends.

B. Complete the Passage

Use the correct form of the word choices given to complete the passage.

million	hotel	Earth	seat	space	star	fly	spaceship

Galactic Suite
The First Space Hotel

Do you want a *really* unique holiday?

Everybody wants to go to 1. __________. At night, we look at the dark sky and imagine going there. Now, you can go on a 2. __________ and stay in a space 3. __________! From your window, you can look at the 4. __________ and the 5. __________ below. You can also 6. __________ around in the hotel. All this costs three 7. __________ dollars. There are only six 8. __________ on each trip, so book now!

Photos: Galactic Suite Design

C. Multiple Choice

Circle the answers.

1. How high is the space hotel above the Earth?
   a. 45 kilometers
   b. 450 kilometers
   c. 40,000 kilometers
   d. 400 meters

2. Where do the space travelers need to train?
   a. In the hotel
   b. On the spaceship
   c. In outer space
   d. On an island

3. How long is the training?
   a. 15 weeks
   b. Three days
   c. 16 weeks
   d. 450 days

4. Which of the following is correct?
   a. Space travel may cost less in the future.
   b. The article is about a trip to an island.
   c. Ordinary people can go to space right now.
   d. The sun usually rises 14 times every day.

Writing

STUDENT BOOK 1

Writing

Task I *Look at the schedule and fill in the blanks.*

Tuesdays	weekends	football	free	every	can	hobbies	love	practice	always

Stan's Week

	Monday	Tuesday	Wednesday	Thursday	Friday	Saturday	Sunday
16:00 – 18:00		Piano Practice		Study		Football Practice	Football Practice
18:00 – 20:00	Study		Study	French Lesson	Talk to Magali		
20:00 – 22:00	Read	Read	Read	Read	Read	Read	Read

I am very busy. I don't have much 1. __________ time. I go to school, and I have a lot of 2. __________. Reading is my favorite. I 3. __________ read before I go to bed. I like to play 4. __________ too. I play with my brother on 5. __________. I also love to 6. __________ French with my friend 7. __________ Friday. She lives in France. I 8. __________ play the piano too. I often play on 9. __________. I really 10. __________ both playing and listening to music.

Task II *What are your hobbies? Fill in the chart and write about them.*

	Monday	Tuesday	Wednesday	Thursday	Friday	Saturday	Sunday
___:00 – ___:00							
___:00 – ___:00							
___:00 – ___:00							

__________________ (Verb + -ing) is my favorite hobby. I __________________ almost every day. I like __________________ (Verb + -ing) too. __________________ (Verb + -ing) is another hobby of mine. I __________________ every week. I usually __________________ on __________________ (days). I can also __________________. I like to __________________ with my __________________. It's fun!

Writing

Task I *Fill in the blanks with the words below.*

vegetables	groceries	bar	free	are	pay	bread

Dear customers,

Buy at Supersavers this week! There are lots of cheap 1. __________. Orange juice is two dollars off. You can save 20 percent on 2. __________. Eggs 3. __________ half price! Buy a 4. __________ of chocolate and get another one 5. __________. Cheese and 6. __________ are on sale too. Come to the store today. 7. __________ less and get more at Supersavers!

Supersavers

Supersavers Coupons

All chocolate 2 for 1

Cheese — 25% extra free

Save $2 on orange juice

Save 20% on every $10 of vegetables

Buy 1 loaf of bread Get 1 FREE

Eggs ½ price

Task II *Your mom leaves you a note. Fill in the blanks and write a list.*

eggs	else	onions	carry	few	some	bottle

Hi!

There is a sale at Supersavers. Please go there in the afternoon for 1. __________ groceries. We need a 2. __________ vegetables: 3. __________, potatoes, and carrots. We also need some cheese and a 4. __________ of orange juice. Get a carton of 5. __________ too. You can get some chocolate for yourself. Can you think of anything 6. __________? You can use the coupons. Your brother can help you 7. __________ the bags home.

Thanks,

Mom

Grocery List

____

____

____

____

____

____

____

Writing

Task I Fill in the blanks.

more	winter	weather	prefer	snow
summer	cold	agree	sunny	temperature

I'm from Moscow in Russia. The 1. ____________ there is warm in 2. ____________, around 21 degrees Celsius. The 3. ____________ is about minus five degrees Celsius in 4. ____________. That's pretty 5. ____________! We have a lot of 6. ____________ in winter. It usually starts in November and finishes in March. Sometimes, the snow is up to 63 centimeters deep! I 7. ____________ summer. It's warmer and 8. ____________ comfortable. I think July is the best month. Most people in Moscow 9. ____________. Everybody likes a 10. ____________ day.

Task II Write about one of the cities.

City: Melbourne, Australia
Weather: warm, dry
Summer: 23°C
Winter: 9.6°C
Most Rain: October, November
Snow: very little

City: Taipei, Taiwan
Weather: warm, wet
Summer: 28.7°C
Winter: 15.5°C
Most Rain: June, September
Snow: very little

In 1. ____________ (city), ____________, the weather is pretty 2. ____________ (adj.) and 3. ____________ (adj.). The best time to go there is summer. The temperature is usually around 4. ____________ degrees Celsius. Winter is a little 5. ____________ (comparative adj.), at 6. ____________ degrees Celsius. It's most 7. ____________ (adj.) in 8. ____________ (month) and 9. ____________ (month), but it doesn't get much snow.

Writing

Task I *Four students share their opinions about computers. Fill in the blanks.*

typing up	nervous	games	works	Internet
fix	lots of	broken	easier	problem

Bill, UC Berkeley, 18

I spend 1. __________ time using computers. I use them for everything. Homework is much 2. __________ to do with computers.

Tara, Princeton, 21

I don't really like computers. They make me 3. __________. My computer is always 4. __________. Life is easier without computers.

Hoyt, Yale, 19

I'm a computer person. I like to 5. __________ them for my friends when there is a 6. __________. Mine always 7. __________ fine.

Arlene, Columbia, 20

Computers are great for 8. __________ reports and using the 9. __________. I don't use them for playing 10. __________ or watching TV.

Task II *Use the correct form of the words from the box to fill in the blanks.*

spend	by hand	busy	a lot	prefer	and	sound	work	seldom	e-mail

Hello! My name is Jane Johnson. I'm very 1. __________ all the time. I often use my computer for 2. __________. I 3. __________ almost 12 hours on it every day. My job is to write 4. __________ play music. Computers make my music 5. __________ better. My dad is a musician too, but he 6. __________ uses a computer. He only uses his computer to check his 7. __________. He doesn't know 8. __________ about computers. He 9. __________ to write music 10. __________.

Writing

Task I Use the correct form of the words from the box to fill in the blanks.

naughty	yard	male	week	friendly	name	call	pet	help	play

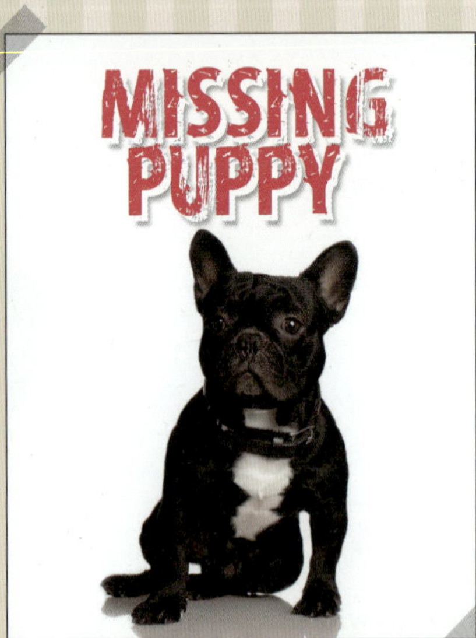

My family's 1. ___________ dog is missing. It's a brown 2. ___________ puppy. He is very smart and 3. ___________ but a little 4. ___________. His 5. ___________ is Spike, and he's around eight 6. ___________ old. He loves 7. ___________ in the 8. ___________. Please 9. ___________ us find him. You can 10. ___________ us. Our number is 055-879-8036. Thanks!

Task II Read the information below and write about the panda.

Animal	giant panda
Name	Gao Gao
M/F	male
Food	bamboo
Birthplace	Sichuan, China — 1992
Lives in	San Diego Zoo, California
Weight	77 kg
Children	Mei Sheng, Su Lin, Zhen Zhen, Yun Zi

Meet Gao Gao

This giant 1. ___________ is one of the world's most famous animals. Gao Gao is 2. ___________ (M/F), and he loves to eat 3. ___________. He is from 4. ___________, ___________ (place), but he now lives in the 5. ___________ ___________ ___________ in 6. ___________ (place). He weighs 7. ___________ kilograms. He has four 8. ___________: Mei Sheng, Su Lin, Zhen Zhen, and Yun Zi.

Writing

Task I *Read the e-mails and fill in the blanks on the map. Draw a line to the post office.*

To: Steve Bright
From: John Geering
Subject: How do I get to the post office?

Hey Steve,

I'm at the office. I need to mail some letters. Where is the post office? Can you help me?

Thanks,

John

To: John Geering
From: Steve Bright
Subject: RE: How do I get to the post office?

Hi John,

The post office is easy to find. First, take a right onto Waleran Street. Go past the gym and then the convenience store on your right. Turn left on Philips Street. The post office is on your left, across from the computer store.

Steve

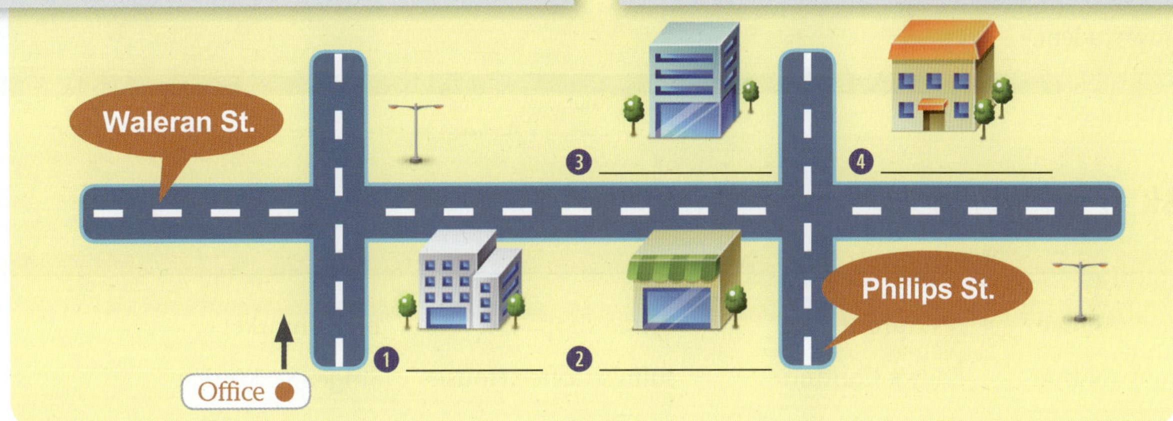

Task II *Look at the map below and complete the directions.*

turn	straight	past	left	right	Kraft	fish	left

A: Excuse me, where is the shoe store?

B: Go 1. ________ ahead and take a 2. ________ on Bridge Street. Go past the supermarket. It's on your 3. ________. The 4. ________ market is on your left. 5. ________ right on Shire Street. Walk 6. ________ the comic book store and cross 7. ________ Street. The shoe store is on the 8. ________.

Writing

Task I *Use the correct form of the words from the box to fill in the blanks.*

cost	study	work	favor	ATM	garage	take	look

GEORGE'S BLOG

About Me
My name is George Buck. I'm from Canada, and I'm a law student.

I'm 1. __________ at the University of Alberta in Canada. My friend is doing me a 2. __________ today. He is 3. __________ me to class. I live far away from the school, and my car isn't 4. __________ again. It 5. __________ good, but it's really old. I need to go to the 6. __________ every week. I should get a new one, but they 7. __________ too much. When I go to the 8. __________ to get money, it always says "zero!"

Task II *Look at the information below and fill in the blanks.*

Place	restaurant	coffee shop	night market
Name	Eddy's Cantina	Julia's Coffee House	Singer St. Market
Where	Main St.	Bali Rd.	Singer St.
Why	eat lunch	meet friends	shop
How often	twice a week	almost every day	every weekend

Where do I eat every day? There are three great places near my house. There's a restaurant called 1. __________ __________ on 2. __________ Street. The food there is wonderful. I have 3. __________ there about 4. __________ a week. It's beside the library, so I like to go there after I study too. When I'm finished eating, I usually go to 5. __________ __________ __________ on Bali Road. My friends and I often 6. __________ there. The third place is the 7. __________ __________ __________. You can 8. __________ there until 11 p.m.

Writing

Task I *Use the correct form of the words from the box to fill in the blanks.*

although	like	way	ocean
pollution	morning	best	peaceful

TOURS OF THE WORLD

Home | Find a Tour Guide | Map | Tours

Welcome to France!

My name is Jérôme. I live in the south of France. It's 1. __________ because there aren't many people here. There are mountains, valley, and rivers. France is a great country. 2. __________ its cities are the most famous, its countryside is really beautiful too. It smells 3. __________ flowers and does not have much 4. __________. I know my 5. __________ around it very well, and I often show visitors the 6. __________ places. You can go walking in the 7. __________ and then swimming in the 8. __________ in the afternoon. You should visit us sometime!

E-mail me

Book this tour guide!

A tour guide for six years!

Age: 28

M/F: Male

Languages: French, English

Task II *Use the correct form of the words from the box to fill in the blanks.*

beach	wait	huge	when	mountain	respect	colorful

Visit Us on Green Island

Green Island is a beautiful and fun place. It is off the southeast coast of Taiwan. All nature lovers must go! There are 1. __________ and beaches. Of course there is a lot of sand too! You can sit on the 2. __________ and swim with the 3. __________ fish. They're orange, white, and black. There are some 4. __________ fish in the water near the beaches. 5. __________ you visit, promise one thing — 6. __________ nature! Don't throw your trash on the ground. That's not cool. I can't 7. __________ to see you!

Photo: Prince Roy-green / Flickr

Writing

Task I *Use the correct form of the words from the box to fill in the blanks.*

or	fail	worry	world	review	report	pass	result

Need to Pass Your Final Exams?

Did you 1. _________ some courses last year? Did you get terrible 2. _________ on your 3. _________? It's not the end of the 4. _________. You can still 5. _________. We can help you organize your notes , prepare a study plan, and 6. _________ for all your courses.

Don't 7. _________ about exams. You can either call 8. _________ e-mail us.

studenthelp@campus.com 055-2341-876
studenthelp@campus.com 055-2341-876
studenthelp@campus.com 055-2341-876
studenthelp@campus.com 055-2341-876
studenthelp@campus.com 055-2341-876
studenthelp@campus.com 055-2341-876
studenthelp@campus.com 055-2341-876
studenthelp@campus.com 055-2341-876
studenthelp@campus.com 055-2341-876
studenthelp@campus.com 055-2341-876
studenthelp@campus.com 055-2341-876
studenthelp@campus.com 055-2341-876
studenthelp@campus.com 055-2341-876

Task II *Use the correct form of the words from the box to fill in the blanks.*

try	last	take	exam	go	don't	be	able	semester

To: Student Help <studenthelp@campus.com>

From: Mallory Archer <mallory@isis.com>

Subject: Exam Tips

Hi!

My name is Mallory, and I need your help! I failed several courses 1. _________ year. I studied hard, but there was just too much work. I 2. _________ lots of classes, and I wasn't 3. _________ to spend enough time on each course. I 4. _________ my best! I had eight textbooks. There 5. _________ too much information! I 6. _________ have a good study plan either. I just reviewed before my 7. _________. I 8. _________ to all my classes, but that wasn't enough. This 9. _________, I don't have so many classes. I still need some help though.

Thanks,

Mallory

Writing

Task I *Use the correct form of the words from the box to fill in the blanks.*

on	next	invite	celebrate	invitation
like	relative	at	decorate	attend

Dear Nora,

This is a(n) 1. ________ to a surprise party to 2. ________ Frank's birthday. It's 3. ________ November 13th. That's 4. ________ Saturday. Can you 5. ________ the party? It starts 6. ________ eight p.m. I 7. ________ all of his friends and 8. ________! Would you 9. ________ to help me? You can come earlier and help 10. ________ the house.

Get back to me as soon as you can!

Your friend,

Emma

Task II *Use the correct form of the words from the box to fill in the blanks.*

free	dress up	interested	at	invite	band	formal	able	play

Dear Emma,

Thank you for 1. ________ me! I am 2. ________ that Saturday. What should I wear? Is it a(n) 3. ________ party? Should I 4. ________? I'm 5. ________ to be there 6. ________ six p.m. I can help you get the house ready and prepare the food.

Would you be 7. ________ in having a(n) 8. ________? I heard a good one a month ago, and I can invite them to 9. ________ at the party.

Thanks!

Nora

Writing

Task I *Use the words from the chart to fill in the blanks.*

WHAT RONALD EATS

Meal	Food	Place
breakfast	sandwich	park
lunch	salad and fries	university restaurant
dinner	green vegetables and rice	Julio's

I eat at the same places every day. For breakfast, I make a cheese **1.** __________ at home and bring it to the **2.** __________. I have **3.** __________ at the **4.** __________ restaurant. There is a good **5.** __________ bar, so I often eat a large salad and **6.** __________. The restaurant is just beside my classroom, and the people there are friendly. For dinner, I eat at **7.** __________. It's a small restaurant near my house. I usually don't order much meat because I'm trying to lose weight. I just eat **8.** __________ vegetables and brown **9.** __________.

Task II *Write **H** for healthy foods and **U** for unhealthy ones.*

soda		cookies		rice		fries	
water		salad		beans		ice cream	
fruit		cheeseburgers		hot dogs		green peppers	

Fill in the blanks. Use the adjectives below and a dictionary.

Adjectives	delicious	terrible	bitter	sweet	sour

What __________ (your name) Eats

My favorite food is __________. It's / They're __________ (adj.). I also like to eat __________ and __________. I love __________ too. It's / They're bad for me, but it's / they're __________ (adj.). My least favorite food is __________. I really don't like it / them. It's / They're __________ (adj.). I'd like to eat more __________ because it's / they're really healthy.

Writing

Task I

Read the e-mail. Use the correct form of the words from the box to fill in the blanks.

fish	abroad	tour group	independent	tour	anywhere	visit

From: henrystanley@rowlands.com
To: info@travel.com
Subject: Travel Plans

Hi!

I plan to travel 1. ________ this August. I don't want to go 2. ________ cold. I'd like to 3. ________ Africa. I'm not an 4. ________ traveler. I want to go with a 5. ________. I love 6. ________. Can I have some information on your 7. ________, please?

Thank you,

Henry Stanley

Task II

Use the information below to complete the reply.

Selous Travel Tanzania (12 days)

Activities	
sailing, fishing, swimming	
Airport	
Dar Airport	
Flights	
Arrive	*Leave*
Time: 10:40 a.m.	Time: 3:20 p.m.
Date: July 14th	Date: July 25th
Hotel	
Ras Kutani	

Other words to use:
travel / going to / contact / terrific / guide / relax

From: info@travel.com
To: henrystanley@rowlands.com
Subject: Re: Travel Plans

Dear Mr. Stanley,

We have a nice tour in Tanzania, Africa. It's 1. ________ be the best one of your life. You are going to fly into Dar 2. ________ on 3. ________ 14th. You stay at the hotel for two days and then 4. ________ to the Selous Camp. Our 5. ________ can show you some 6. ________ places for fishing. The camp is great for sailing and 7. ________ too. After six days, you go back to the hotel. There, you can 8. ________ and write a few postcards.

Please 9. ________ us for more information.

Kind regards,

George

Travel.com

NOTES

NOTES

NOTES